Global Business

Mahesh K. Joshi is a senior executive with more than three decades of experience in leading and growing global businesses. He has managed businesses across the globe, and his skill sets include building global and regional strategies and working across multiple geographies and cultures to build enthusiastic and energetic high-performance teams.

Mahesh has held leadership roles in several multinational companies including Ingersoll Rand (NYSE: IR) as a General Manager, Cameron, a Schlumberger (NYSE: SLB) company, as the President of Centrifugal Compression, and CIRCOR International (NYSE: CIR) as the President of Energy Group. He has also held several board positions across the world in various companies, and is currently the Chief Executive of valve business at Larsen and Toubro (NSE: LT).

Mahesh has a Master's degree in International Strategy and Diplomacy from London School of Economics, an MBA from Murray State University, and Bachelor of Science in Mechanical Engineering from Delhi Technological University. He is a graduate of The Advanced Management Program at Harvard Business School, and Oxford Advanced Management and Leadership Program at University of Oxford, where he was bestowed the honour of Outstanding Alumni Award from the OAMLP, Saïd Business School, University of Oxford in 2017.

Mahesh is the also the host of popular business show *Global Business with Mahesh Joshi* on the VoiceAmerica network, which has attracted large number of listeners and downloads from across the world.

J.R. Klein is the Principal of J.R. Global, LLC, a consulting firm dedicated to facilitating global transformation through local initiatives that strengthen markets by addressing barriers to access. His focus is the systemic change in the areas of water, energy, education, and health. He specializes in the revival of local communities by centering on visionary leadership, business climates, workforce development, and public/private collaboration. He is also the CEO Emeritus of Finance Fund, a state-wide social impact financial institution in the USA, growing assets from $50,000 to nearly $400 million.

He has presided over business and social impact initiatives with investment of more than $3 billion in local business, education, health care, community facilities, and affordable housing. He has served on the board of the National Children's Facilities Network, Community Reinvestment Fund, Community Development Finance Institution Coalition, New Markets Tax Credit Coalition, New Markets Tax Credit Fund, Inc., Business Loan Conduit, LLC, Dudley Ventures Community Investment, Huntington National Bank NMTC Advisory Board, and the JPMorgan Chase National Community Advisory Board.

J.R. completed an MBA and has continued his post-graduate education at the Harvard Business School and Saïd Business School at the University of Oxford, and has been awarded three Master's level qualifications: Performance Measurement (HBS), Strategic Prospectives (HBS), and Advanced Management and Leadership (Oxford).

Global Business

Mahesh K. Joshi and J.R. Klein

OXFORD
UNIVERSITY PRESS

OXFORD
UNIVERSITY PRESS

Great Clarendon Street, Oxford, OX2 6DP,
United Kingdom

Oxford University Press is a department of the University of Oxford.
It furthers the University's objective of excellence in research, scholarship,
and education by publishing worldwide. Oxford is a registered trade mark of
Oxford University Press in the UK and in certain other countries

First Edition published in 2018
Impression: 1

Published in the United States of America by Oxford University Press
198 Madison Avenue, New York, NY 10016, United States of America

British Library Cataloguing in Publication Data
Data available

Library of Congress Control Number: 2018931546

ISBN 978-0-19-882748-1

Printed and bound in Great Britain by
Clays Ltd, Elcograf S.p.A.

Foreword

At Said Business School, we pride ourselves on being a "world-class business school, embedded in a world-class university, tackling world scale problems." One of our premier offerings is our Oxford Advanced Management and Leadership Programme (OAMLP), which assembles a global class of seasoned executives guided expertly in the last years by Dr. Lalit Johri. The programme leads participants to think deeply about themselves, their careers and lives, their organizations, and their purpose. True to our mission, it also challenges them to think ahead and beyond, to ponder the global challenges facing our world, and to contemplate the role that they and Oxford can play in addressing these challenges.

Global Business by Mahesh Joshi and J.R. Klein is a result of that provocation. Coming from different backgrounds they met in Oxford, and their partnership of critical thinking produced the book you are about to read. Despite its title of "Global Business," the book not only deals with global trends in business, but also their drivers and consequences. It moves freely between macro-forces to details by country, technology, and organizational form. It is an expansive look at the world today, seen through the lens of globalization.

There are two valid competing narratives today, caricatured by the opening of Dicken's 1859 A Tale of Two Cities:

> It was the best of times, it was the worst of times, it was the age of wisdom, it was the age of foolishness, it was the epoch of belief, it was the epoch of incredulity, it was the season of Light, it was the season of Darkness, it was the spring of hope, it was the winter of despair, we had everything before us, we had nothing before us, we were all going direct to Heaven, we were all going direct the other way—in short, the period was so far like the present period, that some of its noisiest authorities insisted on its being received, for good or for evil, in the superlative degree of comparison only.

The judgment that we are living in the best of times is reflected in the subtitles of books like Steven Pinker's Enlightenment Now: The Case for Reason, Science, Humanism, and Progress; Peter Diamandis and Steven

Kotler's Abundance: The Future Is Better Than You Think; and Hans Rosling, Ola Rosling and Anna Rosling Roonlund's Factfulness: Ten Reasons We're Wrong About the World—and Why Things Are Better Than You Think. These books marshal evidence to demonstrate that on many dimensions that the world has never before delivered as good a quality of life to so many human beings. Collectively, these works see the future as largely positive, with technology, entrepreneurship, and reason leading us to future improvements in well-being.

The case for the worst of times, or at least a more tempered view of the future, can be found in Kate Raworth's Doughnut Economics or in the report by Dennis Pamplin and Stuart Armstrong, Global Challenges—Twelve risks that threaten human civilisation—The case for a new category of risks. In these assessments, while we have made great progress, the benefits of technology and globalization are spread unequally, our planet is in grave threat, and the very technologies which we hope will save us have the potential to be weaponized and lead to our destruction.

These divergent viewpoints have legitimate bases in fact. We may be living in the best of times so far, but sowing the seeds of our own and our planet's destruction. We may be living in bliss, but with our hubris building a Tower of Babel that will divide us, not just linguistically as in the Bible story, but also culturally and worse, perhaps make our world unliveable.

It is in this complicated territory that Joshi and Klein offer us Global Business. The lack of a subtitle reflects the balance of the book. They navigate between different points of view, discuss new technologies, new cultural mind-sets, new organizational forms, and economies on the rise—China, India, Africa, and Australia. They discuss threats to local businesses, changes to the way we will work, how we manufacture products, take care of our health, move from place to place, and more. Surely, some of these predictions will take place sooner, and others later, and some not at all—perhaps taken over by innovations yet to be conceived.

Throughout all of this, I go back to the programme that brought Joshi and Klein together—a programme designed to help us learn how to better manage and lead. How will we manage the technologies that can either improve our lives or lead us to destruction? How will we lead people and organizations through this more complicated global world? What skills, capabilities, and attitudes will serve leaders well? How will business, government and civil society work together constructively? While innovation may drive continued prosperity, how do we ensure that the decentralized adoption of new technologies doesn't permit unscrupulous uses that impose costs and externalities on us all? Posing the right questions is the first step to answering them. Oxford has always stood for independent and critical thinking, but the world demands thought *and action*. Global Business not only enhances our ability to understand the world, but also to help leaders chart the course to our continued collective well-being.

Professor Peter Tufano
Peter Moores Dean
Saïd Business School
University of Oxford
www.sbs.oxford.edu

Preface

I got a haircut last night. It has been some time since a haircut was a notable event for me. At a certain point when I was growing up, it ceased qualifying as an event and became a brief encounter resulting from necessity. My barber has lived with me for more than 49 years and in her spare time raised a family, and kept me from wandering away. The brief encounter took place in the bathroom and was highlighted by only three brief words, "there you go." Before I had a personal barber I would go to the "barber shop" where I would listen to the pulse of the American republic. Conversations filled with local gossip, the day's news stories, politics, always politics, were more the attraction of the place than actually getting a haircut. Many fervent, at times heated, discussions were held with one side under the sheet and the other with a pair of scissors in hand. At the end of the heated discussion the scissors were put away, the sheet was removed, the bill was paid, hands were shaken, and we parted friends. The process was an essential typology of democratic capitalism, it was relevant, and it was civil.

This trivial lesson learned is the frame of how this book came to life. The world into which we all have been born is more complex and confusing than it has ever been. So when I was given the opportunity to attend the University of Oxford Said Business School Advance Management and Leadership Program (OAMLP), I embraced the prospect of thoughtful clarity. The experience provided an opportunity to build relationships with people from all round the globe who were looking for more or less the same things I was—a bit of clarity, thoughtful dialogue, and celebration of common civility. It was there that I met Mahesh Joshi and began a friendship driven by a mutual respect and shared purpose.

Our backgrounds were similar, yet vastly different. We were both products of thought- driven environments that prioritized thinking through problems, devising strategies, and implementing solutions. We shared basic values and curiosity about the changing world and its perceived lack of understanding by most people regardless of origin but with common destinies. Mahesh's Masters in International Strategy and Diplomacy from the London School of Economics, MBA from Murray State University in the United States, and a Degree in Mechanical Engineering from India gave him a unique perspective and worldview. My career in social impact finance and inclusive capitalism (as it is now called) put me firmly in the non-governmental organization world for more than 40 years. When we met, we not only shared our passion but some of the same experiences at Oxford and Harvard, which we both attended as postgraduate scholars.

Oxford's OAMLP provided a caldron that stirred ideas, scenarios, and possibilities. The experience was enabled and enhanced by the mentorship of Dr. Lalit Johri, Senior Fellow in International Business at Saïd Business School and Director of OAMLP. It was Lalit that first suggested we do something globally together. It was Mahesh's initiative to build and host a radio program on VoiceAmerica ("Global Business with Mahesh Joshi") and I was honored to contribute to that venture. It was that program which led to the next logical step. How could we reach more people with a simplified message about globalization and provide an unbiased explanation of what is happening around us? This book is the beginning of that agenda.

We gratefully acknowledge the contribution of OAMLP's staff, educators, and coaches. Special thanks are due to Dr. Johri, Dr. Sue Dobson, Associate Dean of Faculty at Saïd Business School and a Fellow of Green Templeton College, and Dr. Andrew White, Associate Dean for Executive Education and Corporate Relations at Saïd Business School and Fellow of Green Templeton College for their help and encouragement. We are eternally grateful for the formal and informal discussions and dialogues with our OAMLP colleagues from our class of 2014, and for all the other individuals who have listened, advised, and encouraged this effort. It would also be remiss of us not to mention the invaluable contribution of those who participated in the "Global Business with Mahesh Joshi" program. It was their contribution, their thinking, experience, perspective, and expertise that inspired us.

J.R. Klein
Principal, J.R. Global, LLC
CEO Emeritus, Finance Fund

Acknowledgment

Global business and international trade were once considered the bastion of large corporations who had the resources and financial muscle to become multinational companies. The advent of digital technology connected the whole world and made it without boundaries for business. The shipping lanes lost its prominence to broadband. The internet allowed a small business in Paducah, Kentucky, an artisan housewife in a remote village in Kenya, an entrepreneur in Yantai, China, and a coppersmith of Almora, India, to connect with the whole world and get noticed for their products. Technology leveled the playing field at a phenomenal pace. I had the unique privilege of experiencing it first hand over the past three decades while working with multinational companies in various geographies from a developing economy in Asia to a developed economy, USA. Extensive business travels to more than 40 countries across the globe, living on three different continents, and running businesses in several countries provided a fascinating learning experience.

I can't thank enough the several thousands of my colleagues at work in various cities across the globe, customers, suppliers, peers, leaders, cab drivers, hotels staffs, fellow passengers on domestic or international flights for enriching my knowledge and understanding of global business with touch of numerous cultures, inspirations, problem solving capabilities and methodologies.

I had the opportunity to work with several very effective business leaders across the globe coming from different countries and cultures that helped to develop a global thought process. The initial phase of working with an American multinational Ingersoll Rand India exposed me to business leaders who provided the expertise on how a multinational company from a developed economy can successfully operate and grow in underdeveloped countries. The next level of exposure came in the USA working at the business headquarters of Ingersoll Rand and it provided another set of valuable lessons under the leadership of Tommy Nilsson on how to manage global business with precision across different cultures, Ted Doheny on how to strategize and execute in a global environment while building networks, and Darius Adamczyk to think fast and execute to perfection with quality, precision, and speed for different market needs across the globe with a clear and well-defined strategy to be the market leader. I had an opportunity to work with leaders like Jack Moore at Cameron who personified the expertise of motivating people across the globe to give their peak performance. It will not be out of place to say that I also had the opportunity to learn from several other leaders on what not to do to succeed in global business. All the learnings are reflected in the book presented to you as a product of my journey into the crucible of learning businesses across the globe.

I also feel lucky to have had exposure to not only the practitioners across the globe but also the academics across the world in pursuit of my continuous learning endeavours. My educational journey, starting with schooling at Ramjas School in New Delhi in India, was followed by engineering education at Delhi College of Engineering in New Delhi, continued with management education at Nirma Institute of Management in Ahmedabad, India, and Murray State University in the USA. These impacted my learning process in the formative years. The journey through the Harvard Business School, Oxford University and London School of Economics taught me that there is no end to learning, and there are various solutions to the world problems. These are all wonderful temples of learning which shape your thought process in a very constructive and positive manner to make you a better human being and to do something to make a difference in the lives of fellow human beings. Meeting Prof. Nitin Nohria, Ranjay Gulati, Cynthia Montgomery, Guhan Subramanian, Richard Vietor, V.G. Narayanan, Rajiv Lal, Ananth Raman, and Marc Bertoneche at Harvard Business School and Lalit Johri, Andrew White, Sue Dobson, and Peter Tufano at Oxford made me understand the finer points of leading successful businesses across the world. The interactions with Prof. Michael Cox, Christopher Coker, Gordon Barrass, Sir Robert Cooper, Jonathan Powell, Luca Tardelli, Nick Kitchen, Barry Buzan, and Danny Quah, at London School of Economics, provided the much-needed insights into the impact of geopolitics and international relations. The classmates in these institutions also enriched quality of my learning.

There has been a tremendous teamwork in the Klein as well as Joshi family. Lola Klein provided support and constant encouragement to James and I, right from the day we attended Oxford together. My in-house think tank, my wife Anita, and kids Pranav and Shaguna, contributed to the development of intellectual content for my radio show as well as the book and participated in long, interesting and thoughtful discussions. I am also thankful to all the people who have contributed to the development of this book and I have missed to mention them here.

This book has been written to provide a simplified understanding of a very complex subject. It is supported by years of learning in global markets by the practitioners and the thought process influenced by the experts on the subject in academics.

Mahesh K. Joshi
Chief Executive
Larsen and Toubro Valves
Host: "Global Business with Mahesh Joshi"
VoiceAmerica.com, Business Channel

Table of Contents

Table of Contents

Part I
The World Today

1

Global Impacts from the White House to a Kenyan House

To begin our thinking about the state of a globalized world, it is important to set the basic foundation for such thought. Our look at globalization and world economics will draw on some of the best minds in the world of global and economic thought. It is our aim to present the sophisticated and complex truths of globalization in a way that is understandable and palatable. The initial chapters will examine a perspective of the world that is not always accessible or even acknowledged by business, governments, or individuals. This stage will be used throughout the book to frame the basics of discussion.

In the past several decades global business has created unprecedented growth in the global economy. The increase in world population and in the number of nations since the middle of the twentieth century has fueled consumption and created new channels for trade. The rising trend in global trade is not just in products and services but also in knowledge, investment, and people. The evolution of technology, at a pace never seen before, has connected the whole world seamlessly to further enhance global trade, with easy access to customers and suppliers. Despite the growth generated by global business, globalization remains a hot topic with some segments of society trying to promote protectionism and create rhetoric in favor of anti-globalization. The combination of trade channels already in place, cross-border trade by most countries, support from internet technology, and the connectedness of the whole world has continued to support global business till now.

Accelerated Globalization Enabled by Technology

The internet and other technological advancements are playing, and will continue to play, an increasingly important role in terms of delivering almost every human requirement, that is, education, health services, global awareness, accessibility, distribution, and knowledge. A World Bank study found that if there was a 10 percent increase in broadband penetration in a developing country, it resulted in a 1.38 percent increase in growth. Similarly for developed countries there was an almost 1.21 percent increase for every 10 percent increased broadband penetration (Minges 2016). As these statistics suggest, there is an observable phenomenon that links internet access to rising income and living standards for people in the framework of globalization and international trade. Another positive impact is technology transfer, which means better products are available to customers in more countries. Transferring the technology through different mechanisms tends to bring down the cost without compromising the quality of the product. Technology driven through mechanisms such as the internet comes with an expectation of further evolution in global trade.

Many start-up companies, when asked, "How good is your accessibility to the market?" immediately point to an e-commerce model that allows access not only to otherwise inaccessible local, rural markets but also to overseas markets. E-commerce is a powerful tool for individual entrepreneurship and also many large corporations that use e-commerce or e-business for international marketing of their products and services. It is impressive to think about how e-commerce and technologies are empowering individuals and entrepreneurs, and technocrats. Businesses find it much easier to communicate with their audiences, locally and around the world, using the power of internet and information technology.

E-commerce is emblematic of the positive impact of technical innovation on the global market. Sectors like the entertainment industry are exploiting the power of the internet. Technology is definitely impacting international trade with many international organizations developing new products and services to suit the taste of customers in emerging economies. As a result consumers can now select products that suit them. These products are designed for the domestic consumer and, as a result of reverse innovation, are not necessarily very expensive. There are many cross-border strategic alliances and public/private partnerships that focus on research and new product development. Technology is playing a powerful role in international trade, international product development, and even the development of new solutions to benefit society and provide better goods and services for the human race as a whole.

Drivers of Global Business

The world population has increased from 2.5 billion in 1950 to 7.2 billion in 2015 and the number of member states in the United Nations has grown from

60 to 193 in the same period (United Nations, no date) (UNCTAD 2016). The tripling of nation-states has also increased the number of possible trade channels available to each country and the volume of commerce has increased from $62 million in 1950 to $19 trillion (UNCTAD 2016). Several other factors, in addition to population, have contributed to the growth in global trade.

The Drivers of Growth

There are three fundamental drivers of the increase in global business. First, there are more consumers on the planet at around 7.2 billion and growing (UNCTAD 2016). These consumers want more products, they want cheaper products, and they want better products and services to improve their lifestyle. In addition a lot of these consumers are from emerging markets, where the income and purchasing power of households is increasing, thereby creating a surge in demand for products and services. Sixty-six percent of the growth in trade is now coming from these emerging markets (UNCTAD 2016). They are becoming the key drivers of the increase in international commerce and are also the main contributors to the growth of the global economy. More than 50 percent of future growth in the world economy will come from growth in emerging markets (UNCTAD 2016).

The second driver is, with an increase in demand beyond the home markets, many international and global companies are expanding their operations in foreign markets. These companies import and export enormous amounts of knowledge, investments, goods, and services throughout various business processes, thereby fueling growth in trade. The evidence of this is an increase in international trade as a result of growing trends in terms of bilateral, multilateral, and free trade agreements between and amongst countries. These free trade agreements are the final reason for the increase in global trade. The easing of trade barriers and the willingness of governments to work together has opened cross-border trade and made it easier.

The third driver is the growth of the number of middle-class consumers in emerging markets. There were about 3.2 billion people in the middle class at the end of 2016, and with the current pace of growth of that class, in the next few years a majority of the world's population will be middle class and above. The majority of the new middle class is coming from Asia. The global middle-class market can be divided into a slow-growing, developed-country middle class, and a fast-growing, emerging-economy middle class. There are also geographic distributional shifts in the market as two Asian emerging markets, namely, China and India, are accounting for a large market share, whereas the European and North American middle class is currently stagnating

5

(Kharas 2017). Growth in the number of consumers (particularly middle-class consumers in emerging markets), the global expansion of international and worldwide companies (particularly their supply chain), and the falling of trade barriers have all enabled the recent increase in global trade. These are primarily people-based, which logically brings the focus to China and India, but there is another aspect that deals with the movement of people or talent across borders.

The Talent Impact

The employment and movement of talent from country to country is a form of exchange and this is a new dimension regarding internationalization and growth in international trade. In some countries there is a shortage of talent and in others a surplus of skilled labor, combined with an inability to create enough jobs. India is a classic example of this, with so much talent that engineers and software designers must find work in other countries. It is difficult for the domestic economy to provide these types of job opportunities. This is a new trend that has become increasingly evident in the last two decades. Cross-border movement of talent is positive for the human race. It improves levels of awareness, provides an opportunity for cross-national cooperation, and strengthens trade ties between countries.

The Exporter

In today's economy China is the world's largest exporter of goods, with almost $2.2 trillion in exports, and the United States is the world's biggest importer at $2.3 trillion (WTO 2017). How would a cessation of global trade impact these countries? The importance of global trade is undeniable as it is impossible to meet a country's internal consumer demands without relying on a significant amount of trade. Thus, the disruption in global trade would have catastrophic effects. China has recorded ever-increasing rates of economic growth in the last three decades fundamentally based on their "export push." The Chinese Government has provided every kind of available resource and advantage to Chinese companies including the creation of special manufacturing and export zones. China is acquiring a reputation for manufacturing cheap goods and services for the world. The Chinese economy has to grow in a sustained way recording ever higher rates of gross domestic products (GDP) growth, driven by export. If Chinese exports fall because of disruptions in trade there is a real danger that thousands of workers will lose their jobs, with the consequent rise in unemployment leading to internal instability.

The Impact of Disruption

US households have benefited in terms of large-scale imports of competitively priced products from China. If the trade between the two countries ceases then the supply of low-priced products will fall and consumers will have fewer products to choose from at higher prices. The disruption would affect American manufacturing procurement programs that depend heavily on parts and materials supplied by China. There would be a myriad of adverse effects of disruption in the supply chain. The deeper consequences would be in the currencies and exchange rates. Any interruption in the supply chain, any disruption in the labor market, or any disruption in the living standards of people is bound to have an adverse impact on American society. The breakdown in trade would trigger a breakdown in business processes, the value chain, leading gradually to a multiplier effect. The shockwaves would travel right down to the society level, the household level, and the individual level. It would potentially reverse the developing country trends and drive millions of people back into poverty. A trade disruption would require a massive effort to restore the trust and trading relationships that would be an incredibly difficult re-negotiation, and could potentially take ten, 20, or even 30 years.

Benefits of Global Business

Global trade has definitely reduced costs, but additionally, as people have started interacting across the planet, they have learned more about different cultures and there has been an increasing exchange of cultures. This cultural exchange has made people more aware of how things are done differently in other parts of the world and contributes to global understanding and peace. Global trade is important for society as it has helped to reduce poverty, creating jobs across the globe where there were no jobs for people below the poverty line, and it is probably true to say that it has provided greater global access to consumer goods.

There is evidence that international trade, particularly for exporting countries, has created more jobs, and increased earnings and living standards. In addition corporations are developing new products. A fair amount of growth in co-creation and innovation of new products as a result of companies' partnerships are in the form of alliances or public/private partnerships with government organizations. This type of cooperation at the company level between corporations and/or government organizations creates positive attitudes to trade. They are important elements in the cordial relationships that contribute to peace or stronger bilateral relations. Unfortunately, many other factors disrupt world peace and a lot of these disrupting influences are not necessarily within the control of the trading governments, the corporations who are involved in the process of operating global supply chains, or even the workers who are benefiting from the exports.

What if Globalization Reverses?

Pragmatically, it must be admitted there is evidence that the increase in living standards, and other benefits brought about by the rise in international trade and globalization, are not equally distributed across different segments of society. There has in fact been an increase in the level of societal inequality. It seems that people who have the means to benefit from the processes of free trade and transitive technology, and from new opportunities in the foreign market, realize those benefits faster than those who are not part of the mainstream economy. There is an observable trend that the polarity of economic benefits is growing. It could be argued that this inequity spawns rhetoric advocating for nationalism, isolationism, and protectionism. These ideologies argue for trade wars rather than cooperation. The obvious question is "What are the consequence of this separationist positioning and who really is affected by it?" The answer is short but not simple; everybody.

The countries that are dependent on the export of products and services for economic growth will be adversely affected because their goods and services, including the expatriate talent, will not find replacement markets and therefore there will be compression in the economy. Any kind of compression in economies has its own adverse consequences. For large exporters like China and India, and medium-sized exporters like Latin America and Africa, cuts in exports would cause dramatic difficulties in purchasing power, the cost of goods and services, currency valuation, standards of living, and political unrest. Protectionism hurts importing countries because it gives a false impression that you can protect your domestic industries and the sector economy even though it is not competitive. In the short term there is comfort they can protect themselves but in the long run they are exposed to a significant disadvantage. No matter what the political rhetoric says, living in a sector which is not competitive globally in exports or meeting import demands will suffer the same disadvantage despite their ideology. In today's geopolitical climate this is a hot potato when unemployment or redundancy is blamed on "scapegoats," that is, job losses, immigration, trade agreements. Whether the agenda is personal or civic the debate often becomes political. When politics becomes the dominant feature in an economic domain the situation quickly becomes dangerous. Many countries who need investment in technology, commodities, and manufacturing materials and processes, find that protectionism is a barrier to long-term economic growth and stability.

The Hidden Agendas

Protectionism is not just about taxes and the tariffs. There's a whole range of non-tariff barriers which are now being intriguingly applied by western countries. Many western nations have established non-tariff barriers on food in the form of health standards. Whilst it is admirable to have health standards, farm-level procedures, and quality food processing procedures, making quality products with high price points for export to countries with low purchasing power has the same outcome as a tariff barrier. Tariffs and non-tariff barriers together with procedures, inspections, quality standards, and quotas are methods for importing countries to raise the levels of protectionism. Protectionism enjoys a substantial amount of media coverage and many join the chorus around an election. After the election, when the rhetoric becomes reality, what was being guarded against is exactly what transpires.

There is a definite value in responsible trading. International trade must be undertaken on a responsible basis, with standards of ethics, proper care of the environment, good social models supporting the imports and exports, and the engagement of communities and their citizens. There must be overwhelming support from society to become partners in international trading and to contribute to the economic development and growth of their own country and the rest of the world. Going by the evidence of three decades in China and the last two decades in India, if there is a further surge in global trade, it will create millions of new jobs just by increasing the exports of those countries which enjoy competitiveness in certain industries and sectors and which have the right tools in terms of manufacturing and distribution, and the infrastructure to access the foreign market.

In terms of global business, a few interesting facts should be noted. China is the largest exporter of goods but the United States is one of the largest importers of goods and services, valued at over $2.3 trillion. At the top of the list of most traded products (by dollar amount) are crude petroleum, refined petroleum, and cars. There are more than 50,000 cargo ships in operation and the largest container ship is a triple e-class container ship. For each of those ships, approximately 60,000 tons of steel is needed to build it, it carries 18,000 containers and above all, it can survive a 25-meter-high storm surge (Macguire 2013). These numbers are emblematic of a world connected by trade and one that is trending toward more interconnection and the inescapable realization that globalization is here.

References

Kharas, H. (2017). *The Unprecedented Expansion of the Global Middle Class.* Washington DC. Available at: https://www.brookings.edu/wp-content/uploads/2017/02/global_ 20170228_global-middle-class.pdf.

Macguire, E. (2013). *Maersk "Triple E": Introducing the World's Biggest Ship,* CNN.

Minges, M. (2016). "Exploring the Relationship Between Broadband and Economic Growth." *World Development Report,* 1. Available at: http://documents.worldbank.org/ curated/en/2016/02/25851781/world-development-report-2016-digital-dividends-exploring-relationship-between-broadband-economic-growth.

UNCTAD. (2016). *UNCTADstat, UNCTAD Statistics.* Available at: http://unctadstat. unctad.org/EN/Index.html.

United Nations. (no date). *United Nations Overview, United Nations.* Available at: http:// www.un.org/en/sections/about-un/overview/index.html.

WTO. (2017). *World Trade Statistical Review.* Available at: https://www.wto.org/english/ res_e/statis_e/wts2016_e/wts2016_e.pdf.

2

Is Globalization Killing Local Business?

The fact that the influence of globalization has been driven by dramatic changes is not one of those "blinding flashes of the obvious" that seems to sneak up on us, but in reality is very evident and even predictable. Advances in technology, markets, and environments were as precursors to the big changes we are now talking about. Advances in technology have led to the current global grid driven by information. The primary mission of business is to provide solutions, and this technology explosion has provided opportunities and market applications for those solutions. Local businesses now have an opportunity to move beyond their restricted geography of the past into the global arena with the use of technology. A local store in a remote village in Kentucky has the same opportunity as a large store in London to access global customers. These could be exciting times for local businesses if they use technology to their advantage.

We are a Part of the Global Economy

One clear aspect of globalization has been the drive toward international commerce. Businesses are interlinked, creating a powerful force in the form of a market without borders. The whole idea of globalization is a process in which people and communities come to experience an increasingly common economy, social, and cultural environment. You cannot live in this world and not be exposed to how global it is. Irrespective of whether it is a small community or a large community, unless we are environmentally isolated, we have both feet in the global economy and we are climbing.

Impact of Local Communities on Global Business

Rather than asking "How is global business impacting local communities?" the more pertinent question to ask is "How are local communities impacting global business?" We are seeing an increase in emerging markets that are fueled partly by technology that provides real-time information to previously isolated communities, giving them a voice and turning them into viable markets. We are also seeing the creation and growth of common economic, social, and cultural environments that have an impact on the world business climate.

Because of the "glitz and glamour" of the global concept, often, thinking about local communities is neglected. However, there are some strong voices that focus on the woes inflicted on local markets. Anand Giridharadas of the *New York Times*, in his recent address to the Aspen Action Forum, said:

> The winners of our age may be helping society with their Foundations, but in their business enterprises, the main occupation of their life, they are doing serious harm. They are using political and financial muscle to enact policies that help them "stack up, protect and bequeath the money," they offload risks and volatility onto workers, and the owners of capital are increasingly remote from their communities.   (Brooks 2015)

Avoiding the Isolation Trap

Though there is truth in Mr. Giridharadas' sentiment, there are others that run far beyond the facts. The world has a growing number of "idealogs" and fear mongers that voice their own agenda on the question of globalization. More often than not the strategy proposed is to pull away and hide. The greatest danger to the viability of local communities is not globalization but a retreat into isolationism and protectionism. In the global economy, those people and organizations that are isolated and cut off are at a disadvantage. Ironically, the best way for communities to preserve their local control is to become more competitive globally (Morse 2003).

The role of local communities is to create an environment that incorporates the bottom of the pyramid and inclusive capital principles into their global platform. Macro-economic problems are partially solved in local communities. This is based on the concepts that all economics are local and are driven primarily by the individual consumer.

Rosabeth Moss Kanter (HBS) offers some salient pointers for communities that want to think about their global role. The greatest assets to any business, she says, are concepts, competence, and connections.

> *Concepts* (THINKERS) are leading-edge ideas, designs, or formulations for products or services that create value for customers. *Competence* (MAKERS) is the ability to translate ideas into applications for customers, to execute to the highest standards. *Connections* (TRADERS) are alliances among businesses to leverage core capabilities, create more value for customers, or simply open doors and widen

horizons. Unlike tangible assets, these intangible resources are portable and fluid, and they decline rapidly in value if not constantly updated.

Any given region, therefore, can thrive as a world-class centre of thinkers, makers, or traders by growing or enticing one or more of these assets. Moving to these stages takes visionary leadership, a friendly business climate, a commitment to training, and a spirit of collaboration among businesses and between business and local government. World-class companies keep their supplies of these assets current by being more entrepreneurial, more learning oriented, and more collaborative. They continually seek better concepts and invest in innovation. They search for ideas and experience and nurture their people's knowledge and skills. They seek partnerships with others to extend their competencies and achieve common objectives.

Companies have several ways of deriving concepts, competence, and connections from the communities in which they are located. Regions can be superior development sites for concepts because innovators can flourish there, come into contact with new ways of thinking, and find support for turning their ideas into viable businesses. Regions also can distinguish themselves by enhancing production competence through maintaining consistently high quality standards and a highly trained workforce. And they can provide connections to global networks in which businesses find resources and partners to link them with other markets. Urban centres can thrive as international centres if the businesses and the people who work for them can learn more and develop better by being there rather than somewhere else.

Places can establish linkages to world-class companies by investing and specialising in capabilities that connect their local populations to the global economy in one of the three ways: as thinkers, makers, or traders. Thinkers specialise in concepts. Such places are magnets for brainpower, which is channelled into knowledge industries. Their competitive edge comes from continual innovation, and they set world standards in the export of both knowledge and knowledge-based products. Thinkers count on their absolute dominance in technological creativity and intellectual superiority to ensure their position on the world stage. The Boston area, for example, specialises in concepts—in creating new ideas and technologies that command a premium in world markets. Makers are especially competent in execution. They have superior production skills and an infrastructure that supports high-value, cost-effective production. As a result, maker places are magnets for world-class manufacturing. Spartanburg and Greenville, South Carolina, are good examples of world-class makers: They have an exceptional blue-collar workforce that has attracted more than 200 companies from many countries. Traders specialise in connections. They sit at the crossroads of cultures, managing the intersections. They help make deals or transport goods and services across borders of all types. Miami, with its Latin American and increasingly global connections, is a quintessential trader city. Organisations such as AT&T selected Miami for their Latin American headquarters because of the city's Pan-American characteristics. Miami bridges Latino and Anglo cultures in the same way that

Hong Kong and Singapore traditionally have linked British and Chinese cultures. Local communities must become world class.   (Kanter 2003)

Raising the Performance

Milton once wrote: "O welcome, pure-ey'd Faith, white-handed Hope, Thou hovering angel, girt with golden wings." However hope and good attitudes are not enough. Workers' skills must meet international standards, there must be visionary leadership, a friendly business climate, a commitment to training, and a spirit of collaboration among businesses and between business and local government. Contrary to popular belief, low wages or tax incentives are not the primary reason that first foreign companies are attracted. In the United States, a recent study at Harvard University's John F. Kennedy School of Government has shown that state and other local tax incentives play little or no role in where foreign companies locate their businesses (Auerbach and Hines 1988). Foreign investors sometimes do decide to locate in a particular place if they will get tax credits at home for state tax payments, but generally, business factors play a larger role. Attention must be paid to strengthening local existing businesses. It is impossible to sustain sleepy local companies in an environment in which world-class companies come looking for better technology and skills. The importance of local leadership in establishing communities that are conducive, attractive, and collaborative cannot be overstated.

Local Going Global

Local communities can leverage global opportunity in a changing world but it is about more than bricks and mortar. Bricks and mortar are becoming subservient to the technology. The next "blinding flash of the obvious" is the egalitarian nature of this change. Another way of expressing the strengthening synergy of local and global, is the "everyone" and "anywhere" of the equation. The effect of globalization on multinationals and on local businesses is changing everything. Global businesses must begin to think differently about their role.

While Morse highlights the importance of new markets for the continued existence of high-tech companies, the discourse of digital corporate citizenship creates an enabling environment in which transnational high-tech companies can access new consumers at the bottom of the market. There is a growing body of evidence that points to the conclusion that the development and stabilization of local markets/communities comes more from investment (mostly private) in locally based entrepreneurs rather than public entities/governments.

Iqbal Quadir is best known as the founder of GrameenPhone, now Bangladesh's largest phone company in terms of subscribers. During the 1990s, Quadir stitched together a global consortium that launched Grameen-Phone in 1997 to provide mobile phone services throughout Bangladesh. His innovative scheme has allowed local entrepreneurs—mostly women—to buy cellular handsets with loans from microcredit pioneer Grameen Bank and then hire out the phones, with airtime, to neighbors. Today, GrameenPhone has nearly 1 million direct subscribers, in addition to the 30,000 entrepreneurs whose handsets provide phone access to 50 million people (Isenberg, Lane, and Knoop 2007).

Dean Kamen, the inventor of the Segway scooter, is working on a new way to bring electricity to villages in developing countries. Dean is re-engineering the Stirling engine, originally developed 200 years ago, to generate about one kilowatt of electricity, enough to light 60 small households. Now, instead of some world energy company building a single 200-megawatt power plant in Kampala, the capital of Uganda, imagine 200,000 micro-entrepreneurs, each purchasing a Stirling engine and selling one kilowatt each in their respective communities in rural Uganda (Helman 2014).

Capital Allocation

It is not the lack of capital that is the real barrier to economic growth in developing countries, it is where the capital goes. According to Morse,

> [F]oreign aid to governments in developing countries is based on conventional *"wishdom."* It is more of a wish than a fact that poor countries consistently benefit from capital from rich countries. This aid is *"wished"* by rich countries to achieve 1) geopolitical ends, 2) to support the sale of their equipment and consulting services, and 3) to alleviate poverty. Capital given to *entrepreneurs* creates jobs, economic growth, and, ultimately, improved governance. Capital given to *predatory government* bureaucracies only reinforces centralised authority and strengthens vested interests. The problem is, meeting the first two wishes by aiding governments can jeopardise the third. (Morse 2003)

Supporting small entrepreneurs, however, promotes economic stability and eventually helps satisfy all three wishes.

Public–Private Partnership

Both approaches (private versus public investment) involve the use of capital to bring about social impact, but only the first empowers entrepreneurs from below, dispersing economic influence. Historically, this type of technological empowerment promoted the economic and political climate that gave rise to today's developed economies. Water mills, eyeglasses, clocks, and other productivity-enhancing tools put power in the hands of entrepreneurs and merchants in medieval Europe, creating a countervailing economic force against coercive authorities. In response to entrepreneurs' demands and growing economic clout, authorities made compromises, giving rise to significant reforms such as property rights, enforcement of contracts, separation of the judiciary from the executive, and other checks and balances, creating the fertile ground for economic growth and more egalitarian societies to take root. There is still a need for this type of change in the world today (Morse 2003).

Impact of Corporate Social Responsibility

The ramification of this global change goes both ways and is applicable in undeveloped, developing, and developed markets. Speaking about corporate social responsibility, Anke Schwittay says:

> Corporations can engage the citizens of poor countries in commerce. First, don't just sell: Open factories in poor countries and create jobs. Develop and sell technologies that enable citizens to produce more; sell productivity tools, like cell phones and power generators, not soft drinks and cigarettes. Second, partner with small entrepreneurs, which is increasingly possible because they are becoming connected through information technologies. Third, procurement, data processing and call centres can be moved to poor countries. Basic supplies and things like furniture can be bought there. All of these are profitable moves. Cost reduction and market expansion are always profitable. Locating production facilities in poor countries, partnering with local entrepreneurs, and procuring goods and services there reduce costs. Because buying from poor countries expands their purchasing capacity, rich countries' corporations, in their own interests, should urge their governments to lift barriers for importing from poor countries. All these actions will expand markets. Focusing solely on selling to developing countries is self-defeating. Unless productivity and purchasing power in developing countries are raised, companies in rich countries cannot boost their sales or profits there.
>
> (Schwittay 2012)

Local communities must determine how best to connect world businesses and locals and how to create a civic culture that will attract and retain unrestricted companies. The greatest danger to the viability of communities is not globalization but a retreat into isolationism and protectionism. In the global economy, those people and organizations that are isolated and cut off are at a disadvantage. They are targets for factions who feed on discontent by blaming outsiders, scapegoating foreigners, and urging that barriers be built to stem the global tide. But if communities retreat into isolationism, they are unlikely to solve the very problems that led to their discontent in the first place (Kanter 2003). The best way for communities to preserve their local control is to become more competitive. That means in this latest "rendition" of business and macro-economics, they must be global in thought and practice.

References

Auerbach, A. J. and Hines, J. (1988). "Investment Tax Incentives and Frequent Tax Reforms." *American Economic Review* 78(2): 211. doi: 10.1257/jep.6.3.79.

Brooks, D. (2015). "Two Cheers for Capitalism." *New York Times*, July, 31. Available at: https://www.nytimes.com/2015/07/31/opinion/david-brooks-two-cheers-for-capitalism.html.

Helman, C. (2014). "Segway Inventor Dean Kamen Thinks His New Stirling Engine Will Get You Off The Grid For Under $10K." *Forbes.com*, 14. Available at: https://login.ezproxy.net.ucf.edu/login?auth=shibb&url=http://search.ebscohost.com/login.aspx?direct=true&db=buh&AN=96974932&site=eds-live&scope=site.

Isenberg, D. J., Lane, D., and Knoop, C.-I. (2007). *"Iqbal Quadir, Gonofone, and the Creation of the GrameenPhone." Harvard Business Review* case study.

Kanter, R. M. (2003). "Thriving Locally in the Global Economy." *Harvard Business Review*. doi: 10.1016/S0024-6301(97)86604-6.

Morse, G. (2003). "Bottom-Up Economics." *Harvard Business Review* 81(8): 18–20.

Schwittay, A. (2012). "Incorporated Citizens: Multinational High-Tech Companies and the BoP." *Information Technologies & International Development* 8(1): 43–56. Available at: http://search.ebscohost.com/login.aspx?direct=true&db=buh&AN=75362143&site=ehost-live.

3

Inclusive Capitalism and the Return of Social Purpose

Inclusive capitalism is a hot topic, and for the right reasons, it has been the focus of discussions both in academic and development circles around the world. "The role that business plays in society, and the expectations about the role it should play has shifted dramatically in recent years. Called to a higher purpose, or sensing that externalities can only be ignored at their peril, many businesses are increasingly open to the notion that they have a responsibility for creating more inclusive economic systems" (Tufano et al. 2016). This statement is an indicator of the rigorous research being undertaken on the capital and social impact of global business. This chapter highlights the work of the best thinkers and primary players in the world of global business and economics.

Role of Business

Let's begin thinking about inclusive capitalism noted in the basic statement; "The role that business plays in society, and the expectations about the role it should play, has shifted dramatically ... " (Tufano et al. 2016). The definition of inclusive capitalism is more than a simple set of statements and does not always fit well into casual conversation. The Oxford statement hints at an underlying issue:

> Capitalism is under attack. The financial crisis of 2008, [and] the stagnation of the middle class in many developed countries, and rising income inequality are challenging some of our most deeply held beliefs about how a fair and well-functioning society should be organised.   (Beinhocker and Hanauer 2014)

Capitalism in Economic Theory

The dominant economic theory is neoclassical economics. It assumes that economic agents are rational in their behavior and that consumers look to maximize usefulness/utility and firms look to maximize profits. The contrasting objectives of consumers and firms maximizing utility and profits form the basis of demand and supply theory. Some say that it paints a narrow and fairly mechanistic view of how capitalism works through its focus on the role of markets and prices in the efficient allocation of society's resources. In the past couple of decades some of the basic assumptions of neoclassical theory have begun to come apart. Behavioral economists have significant data which indicate that real humans do not behave rationally. Experimental economists have raised intriguing questions about the existence of utility. That is awkward because it has long been the device economists use to show that markets maximize social welfare. Empirical economists have identified incongruities suggesting that financial markets are not always efficient. The macroeconomic models built on neoclassical ideas performed very poorly during the last financial crisis. The neoclassical view holds that the economy is a constantly evolving, interacting network of highly diverse households, firms, banks, regulators, and other agents. Beinhocker believes that the economy is a complex, dynamic, open, and nonlinear system and has more in common with an ecosystem than with the mechanistic systems of the neoclassical model.

Markets

The implications of this emerging view shifts the understanding of how and why markets work from their distributive efficiency to their effectiveness in promoting creativity. It suggests that markets are evolutionary systems that each day carry out millions of simultaneous experiments on ways to make our lives better. In other words, the essential role of capitalism is not allocation—it is creation (Beinhocker 2013).

Life for billions of people today has changed dramatically from what it was in 1800 not because we are distributing the resources of the nineteenth-century economy more efficiently. It is better because we have life-saving medicine, indoor plumbing, modern transportation, access to information, and numerous technical and social innovations that have become available to much of the world's population. The genius of capitalism, according to Beinhocker, is that it both creates incentives for solving human problems and makes those solutions widely available. And it is solutions to human problems that define prosperity, not money.

Prosperity

Most of us intuitively believe that the more money people have, the more prosperous a society must be. But the idea that prosperity is simply about having money can be disproved with a simple thought experiment:

> Imagine you had the $38,000 income of a typical American but lived among the Yanomami people, an isolated hunter-gatherer tribe deep in the Brazilian rainforest. You'd easily be the richest of the Yanomami (they don't use money, but anthropologists estimate their standard of living at something around $90 a year). But you'd still feel a lot poorer than the average American. Even after you'd fixed up your hut, bought the best baskets in the village, and eaten the finest Yanomami cuisine, all of your riches still wouldn't get you antibiotics, air conditioning, or a comfy bed. Yet even the poorest Americans typically have access to these important elements of well-being.   (Beinhocker and Hanauer 2014)

This is why prosperity in human societies can't be properly understood by looking just at monetary measures, such as income or wealth. Prosperity in a society is the accumulation of solutions to human problems. The measure of the wealth of a society is the range of human problems it has solved and how available it has made those solutions to its people.

> If the concept of growth is to have significance, it should represent improvements in lived experience. If the real measure of a society's prosperity is the availability of solutions to human problems, growth cannot simply be measured by changes in GDP. Rather, it must be a measure of the rate at which new solutions to human problems become available. Growth is best thought of as an increase in the quality and availability of solutions to human problems. Therefore, if prosperity is created by solving human problems, a key question for society is what kind of economic system will solve the most problems for the most people most quickly. This is the genius of capitalism. It is an unmatched evolutionary system for finding solutions. Finding new solutions to human problems is rarely easy or obvious, if it was, they would have already been found.   (Beinhocker 2013)

A reorientation toward seeing businesses as society's problem solvers rather than simply as vehicles for creating shareholder returns would provide a better description of what businesses actually do. It could help executives to better balance the interests of the multiple stakeholders they need to manage. It could also help shift incentives back toward long-term investment, after all, few complex human problems can be solved in one quarter. This is not to say that shareholders or other owners are unimportant. But providing them with a return that is competitive compared with the alternatives is a boundary condition for a successful business; it is not the purpose of a business. Having enough food is a boundary condition for life but the purpose of life is more than just eating.

Democracy and Prosperity

A host of scholars suggest that democracy is the best mechanism humans have come up with for navigating the trade-offs and weaknesses inherent in capitalism. Democracies allow inevitable conflicts to be resolved in a way that maximizes fairness and legitimacy and that broadly reflects society's views. Seeing prosperity as solution-driven helps explain why democracy is so highly correlated with prosperity. Democracies actually help to create prosperity because they do several things better than other systems of government. They tend to build economies that are more inclusive, enabling more citizens to be both creators of solutions and customers for other people's solutions. They offer the best way to resolve conflicts over whether economic activity is generating solutions or problems. Many (though not all) government regulations are created to do just that; that is, to encourage economic activity that solves problems and to discourage economic activity that creates them, thus fostering trust and cooperation in society (Dyer et al. 2013).

Once we understand that the solutions capitalism produces are what creates real prosperity in people's lives, and that the rate at which we create solutions is true economic growth, then it becomes obvious that entrepreneurs and business leaders bear a major part of both the credit and the responsibility for creating societal prosperity. Businesses contribute to society by creating and making available products and services that improve people's lives in tangible ways, while simultaneously providing employment that enables people to afford the products and services of other businesses. It sounds basic, and it is, but our economic theories and metrics do not frame things this way. Today our culture celebrates wealth as the benchmark of success (Dyer et al. 2013). Thinking about local solutions is more a part of core capitalism than thinking about money is the simple definition of inclusive capitalism.

Shareholders' Value Trap

Corporations strategies seldom consider business opportunity inside unstable economies or, indeed, outside of anything but shareholder earning consideration. Any consideration of interaction with underdeveloped countries is usually relegated to marketing and sales. There is, however, ample evidence that emerging economies with their billions of potential consumers represent trillions of dollars' worth of purchasing power. It is also the case that barriers to the low income markets can be overcome with innovative solutions. These solutions are not just opening the market for sales but engaging the local community. Many innovations that engage the poor have come from players outside the mainstream in their industries. Microfinance originated with non-governmental organizations (NGOs), mobile money was developed primarily by telecom companies, and micro mortgage businesses in India are being launched by entrepreneurs and firms with no experience in the housing finance sector. Established commercial banks, on the other hand, are usually saddled with legacy systems, fixed assets, regulatory requirements, and occasionally, mindsets that make it difficult for them to lead the innovation charge in financial services for the underserved (Tufano et al. 2016). Instead of abandoning the opportunities at the bottom of the market, a second look might be in order. It is easy to recount the barriers to engagement again and again but there are some good examples that point to workable solutions.

Consumer cash flow is an issue that many companies overlook in their quest to reduce prices. Low income consumers are not just poor, they live in a state of uncertainty. Confusing need with demand is a common problem among organizations serving the poor. Many firms have wasted time and resources trying to market products that are designed for the poor but that consumers do not want. Although customers are numerous, they are often rural and scattered, and it is difficult for companies to manage the face-to-face (and cash-based) interactions that are typically necessary for building a cost effective distribution business. Channels built for the middle-class and high-income customers, such as agent networks for selling insurance, don't reach the poor, even in urban areas, and extending them can be prohibitively expensive. It is not the cost of the initial sale but meeting service warranties and replacing parts that can be a black hole. Small agricultural suppliers rarely have access to high quality resources (or the credit to buy them), they often lack training, and their output can be unreliable. Furthermore, companies that provide training and other benefits to suppliers may find that the resources have been diverted elsewhere through "side selling." Aggregating and assisting small producers through "contract farming" or other means have been effective in surmounting these problems. To be considered to be on the cutting edge, business must be willing to hang their feet over the cutting "ledge." They must dare to be innovative and do what works.

Business—Problem Solver or Creator?

Thinking back to our discussion on the definition of inclusive capitalism and Beinhocker and Hanauer's work, there must be a reorientation toward seeing businesses as society's problem solvers rather than simply as vehicles for creating shareholder returns/value (Beinhocker and Hanauer 2014). This would provide a better description of what businesses actually do. It could help executives better balance the interests of the multiple stakeholders they need to manage. It could also help shift incentives back toward long-term investment, few complex human problems can be solved in a quarter. The obvious question is, "Don't we have a basic fiduciary responsibility to maximize shareholder value?"

In her book, *The Shareholder Value Myth*, Cornell Law School Professor Lynn Stout explains how, contrary to popular belief, corporate law does not require boards of directors to maximize shareholder value. Stout argues that stakeholder statutes and the business judgment rule give directors the latitude necessary to consider the interests of other stakeholders, such as employees and the environmental impacts on communities, in establishing corporate goals and strategy—even at the expense of short-term profits or share price. She also illustrates how a myopic focus on share price paradoxically ends up harming shareholders and other stakeholders over the long term, since such a one-dimensional approach induces and rewards behavior that is at odds with natural laws that govern all complex systems. Individual companies, industries, and our overall economic system are interconnected with, and nested within, larger social and environmental systems. Based on this truth, it follows that a business can only be sustainable when the systems upon which it depends are sustainable (Stout 2012).

> The prevailing shareholder primacy paradigm that is invoked as the justification for increasing share price by externalising costs and risk is not only inconsistent with sustainability, it is largely responsible for our current unsustainable economic path. (Stout 2012)

Corporate Social Responsibility

A company's purpose, its financial and non-financial goals, and the parameters within which it will operate to achieve them are all management decisions, as is the decision to embark on the difficult transition from a single bottom line to a triple bottom line model; that is, capital, social, environmental. Authentic corporate sustainability requires board leadership in which triple bottom line values become part of the company's ethos, or defining character, and are thoughtfully integrated into corporate governance practices and strategy. Debates about the private sector's responsibility for its economic, social, and environmental impacts have been raging since the dawn of capitalism. What is new is the emerging global consensus that business is the engine of economic growth and international development, and that business can and must play an indispensable role alongside government, civil society, and communities to solve complex, global challenges like hunger, poverty, inequality, unemployment, and climate change. This is the realm of social responsibility. Corporate social responsibility over the years has developed from a simple form of check-writing by companies to a complex set of principles that encompass nearly every interaction a company has with society.

According to a definition from the Corporate Social Responsibility Initiative at Harvard's Kennedy School of Government, "Corporate social responsibility encompasses not only what companies do with their profits, but also how they make them" (Kytle and Ruggie 2005).

Companies around the world, and those who trade their shares and analyze their value, have recognized that corporate social responsibility has inherent value. Research shows that, on average, 30 percent of corporate earnings are at stake when it comes to a company's relationships with society (Dyer et al. 2013). Indeed, when the news broke that Volkswagen (VW) had been accused of cheating emissions standards tests, its share price fell by almost 35 percent in the next two days of trading (Cohen and Muñoz 2016). The VW scandal, among others, highlights the continued failure of companies to engage successfully with the world outside the corporation.

There are some tenets of connected leadership that can help revolutionize the way companies engage with society. First, know your environment. This precept urges companies to arduously analyze macroeconomic environments, public attitudes, and company behavior to recognize early on the issues it might face and the ways this affects profitability. Second is purpose—this is the critical test of sustainability in business. Companies that want to be around for decades to come must ensure that society is at the heart of everything they do. Finally, effectively entrenching concerns about social impact and the societal nature of business within the corporate culture. Finding solutions to today's greatest, global, social problems, from smoking to climate change to obesity, must rely on the resources and innovation of business. The winning companies of the future will be those that successfully redefine their purpose and deploy their best teams in pursuit of these great social and environmental challenges (Dyer et al. 2013).

References

Beinhocker, E. (2013). "A Truer Form of Capitalism." *Democracy* 29: 22–8. Available at: http://www.democracyjournal.org/29/a-truer-form-of-capitalism.php?page=all.

Beinhocker, E. and Hanauer, N. (2014). "Redefining Capitalism." *Mckinsey Quarterly* 3: 160–9. Available at: https://www.mckinsey.com/global-themes/long-term-capitalism/redefining-capitalism.

Cohen, B. and Muñoz, P. (2016). *The Emergence of the Urban Entrepreneur*. Santa Barbara: Praeger.

Dyer, D., Nuttall, R., and Parekh, E.-J. (2013). *McKinsey Survey: External Affairs at a Crossroads*. Available at: https://www.mckinsey.com/business-functions/strategy-and-corporate-finance/our-insights/external-affairs-at-a-crossroads.

Kytle, B. and Ruggie, J. G. (2005). *Corporate Social Responsibility as Risk Management*. Cambridge, MA: Harvard University Press. Available at: https://sites.hks.harvard.edu/m-rcbg/CSRI/publications/workingpaper_10_kytle_ruggie.pdf.

Stout, L. (2012). *The Shareholder Value Myth: How Putting Shareholders First Harms Investors, Corporations, and the Public First*. San Francisco: Berrett-Hoehler Publishers.

Tufano, P., Barker, R., and Johnstone-Louis, M. (2016). *In Pursuit of Inclusive Capitalism: Business and Approaches to Systemic Change*. Oxford. Available at: https://www.sbs.ox.ac.uk/sites/default/files/research-projects/Images/ford-report.pdf.

4

Technological Disruption in Global Finance

Will the currency of the future be bitcoins or cryptocurrencies? With Fintech and other digital ecosystems growing rapidly, what is the future of banks? Technology is fast replacing paper currency with electronic transactions. Finance has become very sophisticated with complex and diversified products. New technology and instruments have enabled growth of global financial assets to more than $160 trillion (Brandmeir, Grimm, and Holzhausen 2016). Geographical boundaries for financial transactions have come down with transactions taking place seamlessly across the globe. Due to the global connectedness of financial markets, any event in one country can impact the whole world instantaneously. The financial crisis of almost a decade ago is still being having an impact in major economies. Financing is being used both as a weapon in the balance of power and as a facilitator of cross-border acquisitions. Governments are competing with tax rates to attract global corporations. Individual investors have the opportunities and tools available for geographical diversification of their investments.

The Role of Finance

The rise of global financial markets has bought both wealth and risk to almost every part of the world. In the twenty-first century the role of financing in global business has taken on a new character. Finance has always been an important part of the international trade and taken on the characteristic needed as times change. In today's environment we see the globalization of companies and economies where finance has become even more important. The role of finance is to help companies find the right funding at the right time with the right characteristics to enable capitalization of their growth. The role of finance is essential because money is like blood. It brings life to projects, communities, countries, and economies and without it the opposite is true. Companies are realizing in this global world that they can source finance almost anywhere. The challenge, and the art, is to identify the best place to find the money and where it will bring life to the venture. Finance not only sustains globalization, it also enables it.

Need for Regulations

Therefore, if finance is a driver of globalization than the question should be, "Is the current infrastructure and architecture adequate to support global business?" Most observers would answer, yes, and do so because of one primary advancement, technology. Today we have a growing technology network that is supporting global business, trade, and financing. While the institutional, legal, organizational, and operational realms are still challenged, markets need to be more organized and better regulated. The development of a better regulatory framework by people who understand markets is essential. There are a myriad of regulations developed by politicians with limited understanding of how markets work. This muddies the landscape and forces the creation of more regulations to try and clean up the mud, but which often end up just making a swamp. There is no argument for not having regulations. Business, particularly finance, without regulation would be a jungle. However, there is an argument for a thoughtful and pragmatic regulatory approach that fosters the development of more efficient markets. From a technological viewpoint, finance has enabled high-speed trading, broadening markets, egalitarian ethos, and increased speed and efficiency exponentially.

Impact of Quantitative Easing

The ramifications of correction of the regulatory quagmire have been felt across the globe. As an example, quantitative easing and deficit financing by governments have had, and will continue to have, a dramatic impact on global financing. Quantitative easing is a technical word that means producing more money. This phenomenon has been pushing money all over the world, first in the United States, then Japan, Europe, United Kingdom, and everywhere else. From a private company's perspective, this looks like it is a positive action. Because of the law of supply and demand, a greater supply of money means that capital should be cheaper to obtain. What has happened with interest rates in many countries is that they have moved into negative territory. Negative interest rates, which from the economic point of view are a bit peculiar, may seem attractive but quite understandably have some negative impact. Money is a commodity. Like any commodity it has to have a reasonable price. If it is too cheap there's a tendency to waste it and/or misuse it. This is what is happening in many places today.

The second problem with quantitative easing and this huge amount of money in the economy is that it is postponing the important structural reforms that countries should be undertaking. Governments ask, "Why should we reduce our deficit if financing is available at negative interest rates?" "Why should structural reforms and improvements be undertaken when quantitative easing makes it simple?" In some larger countries that have reached their structural limits, there are situations where this enormous capital stack is not resulting in good outcomes. Because interest rates are either zero or negative, investors are naturally moving to instruments with better returns and often find that they have to assume enormous risk. Therefore, this money supply is leading to treacherous risk-taking positions in the economy. Understanding the worldwide nature of today's economy has dramatic ramifications. It can be difficult to comprehend the size of the market. The daily transaction amount on the foreign exchange markets every day is around $5.0 trillion (BIS 2016). This money flood washes into almost every corner of the global economy. It is good news for companies as they look for financing because the cost of money is down. But it is hiding potential problems and postpones the solution to the institutional problems of many countries.

Impact of Technology

The world has experienced a massive amount of change. Today the industrial age has given way to the digital age and we are already edging our way to the next age, the Internet of Things. Finance is not immune to change. Financial technology, known as "fintech," has businesses providing financial services by using software and information technology (Sanicola 2017). They provide services just like a financial institution and, by doing so, raise the question, "Will banks be around in the near future?" These types of companies are direct competitors to banks. There are numerous other ways of financing too, like crowdfunding. Crowdfunding makes direct financing requests to people who are ready to finance without the involvement of an intermediary. Start-ups have access to seed money to finance new businesses in several of these types of "institutionless" technological mechanisms.

There are also new ways of making payment transactions. Bitcoin and other cryptocurrencies have created ways of developing new currencies that have the advantages of making transactions faster, cheaper, and eliminating the need for financial institutions. There are issues with these systems but the technological innovations of such things as the blockchain, a database ledger which operates like a distributed network that can register blocks of cryptographically-secure, tamper-proof data with members of a network, is probably one of the big breakthroughs impacting the future, of not only finance, but also business in general (Niforos, Ramachandran, and Rehermann 2017).

Impact of Change in Business Models

Another dramatic change that has resulted from the innovations of the digital world are changes to the balance sheet. On the "industrial age" balance statement you have tangible solid assets. If a bank is preparing to make a loan it examines the machines, the real estate, and land to calculate risk that informs the lending decision. Today businesses have changed. There are a growing number of knowledge companies that have little in the way of tangible assets but strong intangibles on their balance sheet. Looking at intangibles, that is, knowledge, people, brand, and expertise makes it different, and from the old paradigm, difficult to structure investment in new business asset classes. A lender must base lending decisions not on the value of assets but on belief in the intangible, whether they are people, brands, or market expectations. Silicon Valley in the United States has more than 20,000 start-up companies, mostly digital. The knowledge-based industry is expanding in other places like India where the second Silicon Valley is coming to Bangalore. The total number of Indian start-ups has passed 19,000 and they are mostly represented not by bricks and mortar but by knowledge (Gooptu 2016).

Global Connectivity

In global financial markets as they have developed, as long as the market is not isolated, what happens in one place has a direct impact on other locations. The fact that the markets and the business are interdependent makes volatility more probable. What happens in China will have a bearing in the United States, something going on in India might have an impact in London. Interdependency has a clear bearing on global markets. In addition there is a progressive shifting of the center of gravity of economic power from Europe and the United States toward Asia. The development of big organizational markets, such as Hong Kong, Shanghai, Delhi, etc. is currently observable, and geopolitics is becoming of crucial importance for financial markets. Today finance without an understanding of geopolitics has no value. Whether an investor, a corporate finance manager, or a financial worker they must have a real understanding of the political world. For example, sanctions, while obviously a big problem for Russia, at the same time have impact on the economy of the countries who are doing business with Russia. Something which is desirable from a political viewpoint may have an adverse effect on other economic parameters. The instabilities in the Middle East are creating problems of immigration in Europe and in other parts of the world. This is creating potential volatility in many markets. Not too long ago sanctions on Iran have completely prohibited its entering the United States market. However, it was recently published that Boeing is going to sell hundreds of big planes to Iran. Things change fast. What might have been prohibited a few months ago or a few weeks ago, today is allowed and is still evolving. Knowledge and expertise in geopolitics is a must for the exercise of sound finance.

The center of economic gravity is changing. Chinese currency today is becoming one of the key currencies of the world. It is becoming eligible for the International Monetary Fund (IMF) special drawing rights. This means it has the status of a quasi-international currency and is now competing with the US dollar and the Euro. In the future there is a potential for some significant change here. The upshot to global business is that all economies and markets are connected. What is happening in one market could have an impact very quickly on all markets.

Cross-Border Financial Transactions as a Geopolitical Weapon

Regarding the balance of power, financing is being used as a weapon. Global business has shattered all borders—people can trade across borders, and financial transactions happen and money moves seamlessly across borders. That system can be used to regulate the market also by putting some control mechanisms into cross-border trade. Over the past few decades there has been a trend of developed nations making acquisitions in emerging countries but now that trend is reversing. Chinese and Indian investors are looking for investments in Europe, the United States, and other places. Some examples of the presence of these investors are India's TATA group which has become prevalent internationally; the symbol of the French way of life, Club Med, is now owned partially by Chinese; the French car company Peugeot has Chinese investors. This reversing of investment participation, even sometimes acquisition, can be a good trend. The implications for developed countries are that companies are being pushed to be more disciplined and higher performing. If stock prices are going down because of performance, the risk is that investors are coming from all over the world to find value. This means the market is supporting merger and acquisition movement across borders.

Also to be mentioned is the role of the sovereign funds, which are full of money; Saudi Arabia has several trillions of dollars, as do Norway, Qatar, Abu

Dhabi, and Singapore. These sovereign funds have vast amounts of money that can be invested in company shares at the minority or majority share levels. Interdependency and the status of developing countries that are increasingly flush with resources and able to exert substantial purchasing power means that acquisition, investment, and mergers are more likely to happen in the future.

Tax Havens

Another element that adds to cross-border investment is the taxation infrastructure. When taxes are under discussion, conversation generally turns to warnings about, or complaints directed at, "tax havens." Governments all over the world are competing on taxes. Companies use this as a potential advantage. Though the blame tends to fall on businesses that take advantage of the lower tax systems, from a business perspective, it is hard to argue against the logic of reducing expense by paying less tax. There are incidents of fraud, however fraud exists despite the existence of low tax jurisdictions. Control here lies with governments and business cannot be blamed for taking advantage of competitive jurisdictional tax structures. Corporate fiduciary responsibility dictates tax optimization as a measure of cost management. The difference in today's global interdependent economic structure is the ease of opportunity.

Governments have to take responsibility, and those that are competing on tax rates must be aware of their treatment of taxation, in a competitive environment, and seek a balanced tax structure that both meets revenue needs and is competitive in the area of tax optimization.

Future

It is always difficult to forecast the future, and there are as many stories of when predictions have failed as there are of correct predictions. Speculation, on the other hand, is more actuarial in nature.

Therefore, based on observable phenomena and the discussion of global economic change, technology impacted financing, and the interdependency of the market there is a strong trend toward China and India playing a key role in the future of the global economy. The size of these markets is enormous. The projects that have to be financed in these economies are also massive. These markets must become better organized, better regulated, and better managed. As that happens, this combined market will begin to be the dominant world economy.

The development of project financing is becoming extremely important in China and India. Both countries will soon need far-reaching infrastructure projects that require substantial financing. The expertise is already evident and some early examples exist. The metro train systems in Delhi and Bangalore have been developed and delivered on time and on budget. The growing reality of private public partnership suggests there will be incentive and knowledge to satisfy capital and public goals uniting public and private investors in the facilitation of the financing of big projects. Both China and India are developing technological foundational infrastructure that, with better organization, better regulations, and greater efficiency, will propel them to the number one and two economic powers on the planet.

There is a great opportunity for international investments. Investors today are faced with the interesting element of geographical diversification, and there is usually a way to diversify a portfolio not only in different industries but also in different parts of the world. In addition to China and India there are opportunities in South America and Africa. As these countries begin to resolve some of their governance issues they will become stronger and more attractive markets.

Investors will have to understand what's going on in the market and how markets are going to change over time. They will also have to understand how geopolitics are going to evolve. They should appreciate the increased sophistication needed and/or professional advice to assess the capital and political risks of investing. From an investor's viewpoint there are many opportunities for investing in those parts of the world, which come with potential risk. An investor must understand the market before jumping in.

Globalization will also lead to the emergence of truly multinational companies. Today's companies—based in the United States, Europe, China—are multinational regarding locations, customers, and employees but not regarding shareholders. Cross-border investment and cross-border mergers and acquisitions are becoming more prevalent. Companies are going to become more multinational in terms of shareholdings and regarding their equity.

The growing complexity of investing uncovers another important realization. As we step into the future, it will be into a world where there is a critical dependence on professionals with sophisticated knowledge and skills suited for the complexity of the market. Products like enhanced government funds, mutual funds, and products designed for investors who do not need to go into lengthy analyses before investment. Finance has become more sophisticated, which simply means complex. From the world of shares on one hand and bonds on the other one, a plethora of products have been diversified and offered to the market. Professional financial advice will be essential. The upshot of this technological complexity is evident in volume. The global financial assets market is more than $160 trillion, ten times the gross domestic product (GDP) of the United States (Brandmeir, Grimm, and Holzhausen 2016). Global stock markets have crossed the $75 trillion mark and with over the counter derivatives, it was estimated to be around $600 trillion in first half of 2016 (Baccardax 2017). Therefore, small percentage moves in this markets can create, or destroy, vast wealth.

Because of the characteristics of the current interconnected world and the forecast for the future, it is clear that finance is essential. It should be considered a primary tool for sustaining a global economy. However, it should also be understood that finances are far too important to be left to financial people only. Common sense and wisdom must prevail and financial tools should inform decision making. The innovation of the financial industry is vital. Finance needs to help solve problems and needs smart people, energy, ideas, and innovation.

References

Baccardax, M. (2017). *The Global Stock Market Is Now Worth a Record $76.3 Trillion—And That's Terrifying*. USA: The Street Inc. Available at: https://www.thestreet.com/story/14229200/1/global-stocks-are-now-worth-more-than-the-global-economy-and-that-s-worrying.html.

BIS. (2016). *Triennial Central Bank Survey Foreign Exchange Turnover in April 2016*. Basel: Bank of International Settlements. Available at: https://www.bis.org/publ/rpfx16fx.pdf.

Brandmeir, K., Grimm, D. M., and Holzhausen, D. A. (2016). *Allianz Global Wealth Report 2016*. Munich: Allianz SE. Available at: https://www.allianz.com/v_1474281539000/media/economic_research/publications/specials/en/AGWR2016e.pdf.

Gooptu, B. (2016). "Economic Survey 2016." *The Economic Times*. Available at: https://economictimes.indiatimes.com/small-biz/startups/economic-survey-2016-19000-startups-in-india-but-exit-options-remain-bleak/articleshow/51161562.cms.

Niforos, M., Ramachandran, V., and Rehermann, T. (2017). *BLOCKCHAIN Opportunities for Private Enterprises in Emerging Markets*. Washington, DC: International Finance Corporation. Available at: https://www.ifc.org/wps/wcm/connect/8a338a98-75cd-4771-b94c-5b6db01e2797/IFC-EMCompass-BlockchainReport_WebReady.pdf?MOD=AJPERES.

Sanicola, L. (2017). "What is FinTech." *HUFFPOST*. Available at: https://www.huffingtonpost.com/entry/what-is-fintech_us_58a20d80e4b0cd37efcfebaa.

5

The Changing Face of Leadership

Globalization

From a business perspective leaders should reflect the economies, the customers, and the markets they serve. Most companies, though competent in their local market, aren't big enough to quickly expand their leadership team to reflect all the demographic challenges of globalism. Mature organizations that are highly successful should have leadership teams and boards that reflect the markets they serve and the people they lead. Often, companies expanding outside their market, start with management from the culture where the parent organization has built its trust. It is based on a shared understanding of what it means to be a member of that society. There are cultural expectations and not a lot of knowledge of the difference between cultures. Corporate cultures are reflective of the countries in which they are born. Over time as they become more international, they should develop global leaders. This, however, does not always happen because of the comfort level with similar value sets and difficulty in understanding other sets of basic societal values.

Leaders measure themselves and their teams against some basic performance standards. Therefore, having a clear background of kinship and teamwork allows for better trust leading to the likelihood of accomplishing performance standards and goals. As companies mature and acquire some cultural agility and adaptability they find that diversity actually makes better leadership teams. From an organizational perspective, the holistic approach to diversity seems to be more productive. There is one essential element that will cause any performance strategy to sink or swim and that is trust. Stephen M. R. Covey in his book, *The Speed of Trust* says, "Above all, success in business requires two things: a winning competitive strategy, and superb organisational execution. Distrust is the enemy of both" (Covey 2008). For teams or companies to succeed in an ever more diverse global economy it is essential to embrace this axiom. If not, Peter Drucker's famous statement that "culture eats strategy for breakfast, lunch and dinner" will quickly become a reality (RICK 2014).

Creating an Environment for Team Success

Often it can be difficult for leaders to trust people at the outset. The development of this kinship as a background for performance may take an emotional toll. The external pressures to choose a team that is comfortable and secure, with a one-flavored leadership team, may be strong but it misses a vital element. Globalization produces an increasingly diverse multinational labor force and customers, and leadership must acknowledge and embrace that diversity. A leader needs three key components. First, they need to focus on people's capabilities and skills. Their skill must fit the expectations put upon them. Second, the leader must create and manage the energy of the workplace. There must be a delicate balance of expectation, encouragement, vision, and pragmatism that provides a common motivation. Finally, a leader must create an environment that is conducive to success. This means knowing the culture, the people, the team, and the process. As an organization moves into the diverse cultural marketplace there are challenging societal variants. This is one reason to step away from the one-flavor leadership model. What is motivational to someone from a European tradition may not be motivational to someone from an African tradition. The idea of global leadership is being able to adjust and adapt to cross-cultural boundaries in order to get the best out of skill sets and people's energies, and to create an environment in which people will be successful individually, as a team member, and as a business. If leaders approach this challenge from siloed backgrounds and a one-cultural perspective with a lack of sensitivity, and if they are unwilling to change, this will lead to division, misunderstanding, and poor performance.

Managing the Cultures

The basic axiom for culture is that it is what we believe to be true. It is our value set, our yardstick, our measure of behavior, performance, and outcomes. There is natural kinetic dissonance between a culture that values duty, consciousness, and focus on attention to detail and one that has values focusing on spirituality, individual freedom, and relationships. Each judges the other based on their set of values. A good leader accepts and understands the differences and seeks out the common ground, sensitivities, and appropriate relationship between them. Sensitive leaders see the potential, not the problems.

Need for Change in Style

The globalized world has differences other than cultural ones. The technological tsunami covering the globe profoundly changes the way we do business and the way we work. It has its own intrinsic diversity issues. Generational differences are a predominant one. The new young workforce, born into a technological world, is dramatically different from what it has traditionally been. Their view of life is different, their core values are more varied, and their communication styles are definitely more diverse. This generational workforce is more tech savvy, social media focused, electronically connected, and entrepreneurial than any before. In the same way as good leadership deals with cultural diversity, generational diversity is no different. Recognizing the dramatic connectivity and borderless potential of this workforce can lead to yet undiscovered vistas.

A reality of this transformational style is that the traditional corporate leadership style does not communicate well across any of those boundaries. Generational and geographically dispersed companies often move slowly through the diversity forest. Forty years ago, a business union in China ran independently from the business unit in Texas because the technology did not allow anything else. This new paradigm has changed even the thinking about who we are as a business. In this process we must also look at some leadership downsides. With the technology that we have, some would say leadership has the potential to get a little lazy. If leadership is to fulfil its basic skill, energy, and motivational goals technology sometimes can make those tasks more obtuse. For example, something like the basics of communication must establish a hierarchy of contact whether it is face to face, video telecast, Skype, or some other technology, such as voicemail, email, or text. The issue is that whatever the hierarchy is, if it is tipped on its head or split in the middle, it should not become a diversion that facilitates less energy or motivation and leads to less interconnection and inclusion.

Communication

Leadership is designed to maximize the labor of an organization. Again, at the heart of all high-performing organizations is trust, respect, and communication. Trust and respect cannot happen without strong communication. How people talk to each other determines how well their organization will function. All channels of communication have value in their own context. Texting has value, as do phone calls and emails. However, there is a danger of never moving from a single channel. It is easy to get away with verbal communication or to focus solely on it. Focusing exclusively on non-verbal communication, for example, runs the risk of losing the ability to be able to deal with conflict or read intent or monitor potential distractions. Leaders must insightfully manage communications and also the appropriate channels, which are sometimes even more important.

The new business model is much more flexible and flat. However, larger organizations, by necessity, need some type of system to organize and implement the basic process of operations. That is usually hierarchical in some iteration. In these organizational structures, leadership should have a vertical component as well as a horizontal one. There are various discussions of the functional difference between leaders and managers. For our purposes we present a straightforward framing. Leaders decide what needs to be done and managers decide how to do it. In that is embedded the idea that not only leaders, but also managers, possess the characteristics of leadership. Those features, such as understanding, sensitivity, motivation, energy, and skill, will feed into the heart of the organization's leadership strategy and performance goals. This also involves conceptual discussion that leads toward some rethinking of the traditional aspects of "sacred" cows. Leaders fear that the trust they have developed over time might be lost if they do not accomplish those quantitative and qualitative more easily measurable goals; namely, an increase in shareholder value. Most leaders do not take the time to step back and think about what the basic purpose of business really is. In truth, it is not making money but to provide solutions to customers' problems. One of the outcomes of that is the accumulation of capital assets as a product of the process. There is evidence that in the process of problem solving, the level of performance is significantly improved when there is a level of trust, relationship, skill, energy, and positive motivation; that is, good leadership. It is well-documented that relationships are the key to success even in a digital world.

Professional Diversity

Often, leaders tend to think of leadership solely in terms of conflict management. Whether interpersonal conflict, task conflict, or process conflict they all diminish performance. Managing societal culture conflict is another element. Many businesses have not grown organically but have grown through the process of merger and acquisition. The sometimes jarring process of melding separate cultures together is a daunting challenge, both professionally and organizationally. It can be done by applying some of the basic philosophical tenants presented in this chapter. In these processes, as with any larger organizational process, there is a certain amount of necessary professional diversity. The diversity of culture between engineers, lawyers, and accountants, marketing professionals and HR professionals, and gender, race, and religion, and all the inborn and closely held siloes of belief involved can be as daunting as any multinational cultural diversity challenge.

Leadership in this new world is challenging, but it is not an impossible venture. A leader must shed the fundamental bias of their own perception of the world. The psychological term for this is a transformational bias. We have the tendency to see ourselves through the lens of our bias. We tend to see what reinforces our belief and ignore other factors. The recognition, by a leader, of transformational bias and its translation into cultural terms is the blinding flash of the obvious that leads to change. The ability to say, "I do not believe that. But I am going to challenge my beliefs because you see it differently. That helps me to understand what we both have to offer and what we collectively can do."

It is the leader's intuitive challenge to discern the right level of diversity. Too little diversity produces group think, and too much diversity can result in not being able to find enough common ground. The transactional leader will only get to a certain level of performance. Most reward-based systems are still transactional and don't motivate or satisfy most employees. People want something more, and that is why people search for spirituality or other activities that can bring more meaning to life. A leader that helps people to find meaning in skills, energy, motivation, and autonomy will see more engagement, more satisfaction, and more effort in the workplace.

References

Covey, S. M. R. (2008). *The SPEED of TRUST: The One Thing That Changes Everything.* New York: Free Press.

Rick, T. (2014). "Culture Eats Your Structure for Lunch." *meliorate*, June. Available at: https://www.torbenrick.eu/blog/culture/organisational-culture-eats-strategy-for-breakfast-lunch-and-dinner/.

6

The Role of Non-Governmental Organizations

Is there a Common Ground?

The Purpose

Non-governmental organizations or NGOs are non-profit social impact groups organized on a local, national, or international level with a relatively long history. The United States saw groups working for the abolition of slavery during the Civil War. The Crimean War had organized group similar to the Red Cross to alleviate suffering caused by the war. Though these groups were not labeled as NGOs they were involved in the same types of cause-driven activities. The three main drivers of NGOs are first, to relieve suffering resulting from natural disaster, civil conflict, wars, social inequities, and other crisis. Alleviation of suffering has been a key driver in the development of NGOs. Secondly, to champion and defend a specific cause such as abolition, children's rights, disabled, diseased, defense of natural resources, and climate change. The third is the motivation to serve the less fortunate (Werker and Ahmed 2007). Many NGOs are active as service delivery organizations providing a particular service to vulnerable population or needy groups. These NGOs sometimes have contractual relationships with governmental agencies. Not the primary sources of funding, the Government is supplemented by private and philanthropic sources. Most large international NGOs are best-known for their provision of developmental and sustainable aid to international clients.

Structure

NGOs are diverse for a number of reasons. There are small locally based organizations that focus on community issue with limited funding or personnel. National organizations like the Local Initiative Support Corporation in the United States focus on national advocacy and support of communities around the country. With contractual, private, and philanthropic support they work through local offices to provide social services. Organizations like Red Cross and World Vision are large providers of social impact on an international stage. Geography is another diversity factor. Some NGOs are focused locally at the community or even the street or block level, some are state or regional, others national, multinational, and still others international. They are also diverse because of the type of issues they address, such as climate, forest preservation, economic access, or health services. They are called non-profits, not-for-profit organizations, private voluntary organizations, community civil society organizations, social impact organizations, or community-based organizations and are all united under the common charitable purpose banner.

What Do They Do?

NGOs characteristically provide assistance and humanitarian aid. They can campaign and exert exposure and advocacy designed to influence thinking and decisions that change the system. They often work to build capacity by mobilizing and empowering populations through training in technical skills and knowledge. In some cases they provide expertise in a particular technical area by providing specific information or delivering services. Non-governmental organizations may be both simple and complex. They may do one thing and many things. They may be big, small, and numerous with millions of them around the globe. Usually working quietly at the grassroots level, they impact people, cultures, and businesses, to make societies more fit to live in and enhance the lifestyle of people. Their common ground is evident in the fact that they consist of highly motivated and committed individuals impacting local communities and global societies for the good of all.

Growth of NGOs

The evolution of NGOs over the past 70 years has been dramatic. Initially most were relatively small, single-issue, one or two persons, and geography focused. Growth has been gradual and usually internal. They have become more complex, coordinating more with others and creating spin-offs and associates in other countries. Just as there has been an enormous increase in numbers there has been a massive growth in complexity. They are essential as the social conscience, realigning and refocusing our common consciousness.

They often provide major insights and are initiators of the innovation enabling new and better ways to facilitate equity through social impact.

Evolution is inevitable and cannot be avoided. The world is always changing. Circumstances and challenges are always moving targets. Recognition of the complexity and interdependence of global systems and the interconnectivity of globalization is indisputable and should be embraced rather than ignored. The planet has been "re-boundaried" making many issues more prominent in the global discourse and forcing NGOs to adjust thinking and strategies.

Major changes like the end of colonialism, the liberation of countries across Asia, Latin America, and Africa, have significantly increased the number of nation-states and actors on the global stage. The end of institutional communism and the Cold War changed the dynamic between capitalism and communism. The communist world has virtually disappeared and the emergence of the "occupied" movements herald new sets of issues around capitalism in the future. Because of the number of countries, national identities, and players in the global system there is a greater diversification of the interest and perspectives around process, drivers, and goals. The increase in democratic countries and states around the world also increases the demand for rights and voice (UN 2014).

Role of NGOs

NGOs are called upon to respond to all sorts of issues, new and old. The positive impact, confirmed by increased scrutiny, is evidence of their provision of quality services, generation of resources and relationships, and relationships with public, institutional, and governmental resources. The legitimacy of small local organizations responding to local populations is perceived as highly legitimate and representative of the communities they serve. Larger NGOs, however, find it more challenging to manage perceptions of legitimacy and struggle to maintain confidence and support in different markets. The increasing numbers of NGOs create more competition particularly for fundraising. Just as globalization tends to blur national boundaries, so does the multiplication of social impact groups which begin to blur programmatic boundaries.

Thirty years ago types of social organizations were well-defined. Humanitarian organizations were responding to disasters, advocates for development and sustainability, rights and justice issues, and environmental climate or natural resource issues. There were distinct boundaries between different types of organizations. Today those boundaries have become less clear and organizations may do both humanitarian and disaster work, political rights and social rights. Issues now are not clearly definable with varying needs like natural resource management, rights and justice, development, aid and assistance. The boundaries between the issues are less evident and organizations are responding with changes in their thinking and strategy. In today's world it is less likely to have NGOs focused specifically on water but several concentrate on the Nexus; that is, water, energy, education, and health because you cannot talk about one without talking about the others (Sarni 2015). They are interconnected. The challenge is to recognize that issues, geographies, and complexities are bigger than any one entity can address. The logical and reasonable approach must be collaboration. If the goal is to address the global issues across geographical boundaries then collaboration not only with NGOs but also with business partners is essential.

NGOs and Business Connection

Business expectations and strategic thinking are beginning to evolve also. Oxford's Saïd Business School in their recently published report "In Pursuit of Inclusive Capitalism, Business and Approaches to Systemic Change," open with this statement:

> The role that business plays in society, and the expectations about the role it should play, has shifted dramatically in recent years. Called to a higher purpose, or sensing that externalities can only be ignored at their peril, many businesses are increasingly open to the notion that they have a responsibility for creating more inclusive economic systems.   (Tufano, Barker, and Johnstone-Louis 2016)

This concept is often referred to as inclusive capitalism that entails moving business focus from solely shareholder value to a conscious inclusion of social values. This thinking change retains social responsibilities often deferred to NGOs.

The significant increase in the power of the consumer and with the rise of social media, the ability to influence both business and governments affects NGOs significantly. NGOs are working with businesses building strategic alliances that improve local communities and strengthen local markets. Projects like the Nature Conservancy and Home Depot collaborated in Indonesia to combat illegal logging and promoted sustainable timber harvests (Conservancy 2007). These alliances are mutually beneficial and unique to business and NGOs. Through these partnerships the achievement of mutual goals, long sought by both through governments, can be accomplished.

Over the past decades there has been a transformation in many societies. There are more developing countries in the world than ever before. Observation confirms corporate presence, and business system investments in these markets are strengthening not only in local economies but across countries and continents as well. This economic value is evident in growing disposable incomes, an increase in entrepreneurial activity, improved health, education, energy, water, and infrastructure.

Love–Hate Relationship

Relationships are the foundation of the social evolution seen around the globe. For years there existed a perception on the part of business that NGOs had little business sense, financial acumen, strategic prowess, or accountability. NGOs, for their part, had the impression that businesses were focused only on money, were unaware or uncaring, dismissive of the concerns of the underprivileged, and pretty much heartless beasts.

The relationship between them often bordered on hostility or tolerance of the nuisance. The prerequisite of any relationship is a desire to have a relationship. The desire must be bilateral with some shared common ground and goals. Often these commonalities develop through crisis or disaster but they are more effective if developed over time, enabling the growth of trust, understanding, and respect for each individual role. The benefit for both is also fairly clear. Business gets a reliable partner to vet and value the process enabling better decisions when it comes to investing in social impact. The partnership provides an opportunity to season and vertically strengthen their workforce by creating opportunities to volunteer, support, and realize personal value for being part of something which has a culturally significant social impact. Brand perception and reputation are intangible values that can be strengthened through the collaboration and may even filter down to an effect on the bottom line. NGOs' value is seen in the connection to a "different world" that can't help but affect operational capacity, accountability, recognition, and realization that rather than being an enemy business, it is a co-worker in achieving common goals. This recognition leads to other more tangible benefits such as access to funds, donation material, training, executive support, and other in-kind services. There is an osmosis of thinking, ideas, skill, capacity, and expertise that is a natural benefit in mutually collaborative relationships. In the long term there is evidence of the migration of personnel from business to NGOs whether as part of the career path or as senior volunteers.

The Difference in Approach

NGO and business have a different approach to margins. Issues of hierarchy, ownership, and command-and-control are very different, yet remarkably similar. Corporations frame the margin by examining shareholder value. They tend to lose sight of the core purpose of business, which is not solely to increase shareholder value. Business exists to solve problems, which remarkably is the same reason NGOs are in business. Business, at its heart, provides a service or products that solves someone's specific problem and if strategic enough they figure out a way to replicate that solution and provide it to a broader market. The by-product of the solution provision is making money. By contrast NGOs do the same thing but emphasize the solution irrespective of the capital by-product. Any NGO that focuses exclusively on providing solutions will be short-lived because if there's no money there is no mission.

The first step for NGOs and businesses should be getting to know each other and looking for the chemistry. It is good to simply spend dedicated time exploring complementary skills, approaches to work, commonly held values, and a mutual understanding of the nexus of each organization. Both sides of the relationship must understand the commonality of purpose and by-product and clearly define their role in the collaboration. They must also clearly define what the desired outcome of the association is at both the macro and micro level. Some time should be spent on defining the parameters and desired outcomes together with the metrics and methodology for evaluating success. If possible they should not rush, but should take one step at a time and avoid jumping into something that isn't ready. Start with small projects and build on success. Learn from mistakes. Learn from failure and build mechanisms together to resolve differences. It takes time, and patience is a virtue. This is a process of trust-building that requires transparency and willingness to risk.

Joint recognition and acknowledgement of risk are essential. Often risk assessment is focused externally on implementing a certain activity together and reaching agreed upon goals but there are also internal risks. An overnight shift in the market might seriously upset a corporation's commitments that may lead to their having to re-examine partnerships. Those shifts in priorities can come from either party. Mutual risk assessment is critical as is understanding the different pressures and a mutual understanding that those pressures are now shared by the NGO. Corporations face quite different pressures to the NGOs, specifically from shareholders and regulating bodies. It is important for NGOs to understand what is driving decision-making and day-to-day priorities. Communication is essential with clear goals, clear metrics, and specifically delineated responsibilities.

Successful NGO–Business Collaborations

There are some good examples of business and NGO collaboration. Carbon Trust in the United Kingdom is helping the business community move toward a low carbon economy (Carbon Trust 2013). They have helped companies to build their climate change strategies. They provide small businesses with free energy audits and offer no interest loans for energy-efficient equipment. Conservation International helped Alcoa add biodiversity conservation into their environmental policies (Corporate Partners 2013). It also advised Starbucks on sustainable issues related to coffee (Starbucks 2016). In the 1990s the Environmental Defense Fund collaborated with McDonald's and eventually ended the company's use of foam plastic sandwich boxes (Environmental Defense Fund 2010). Rocky Mountain Institute works with companies that are exploring innovative ideas in energy efficiency, transportation, buildings, and power generation. They have also worked with Johnson Controls providing analytical expertise to improve energy efficiency in New York's tallest buildings. In addition they have also worked with Walmart in redesigning the whole tracking system to cut down the fuel usage and with HP to remodel their data center operations making it the world's greenest data centre (Burt 2009).

The key to a good collaboration is to move beyond self-interest. Relationships are bound to fail if self-interest is the primary motivator. It must be recognized that these collaborations go beyond self-interest. Good business is good for society. Healthy societies are good for business. A healthy and educated workforce is good for business, economically secure and active populations become consumers, and that is good for business. That is good for all parties. A good solid building of the relationship between NGOs, business, and the public sector is absolutely essential. To build a global society, to resolve major challenges around the planet, such as climate change, resources, natural resource management, trafficking, and disaster response and migration issues, collaboration is paramount. This is the time when collaborative partnerships between business and NGO will quite literally change the world.

References

Burt, J. (2009). *HP Green Data Center Vision Offers Eco-Friendly Power, Cooling Technology*. California: eWeek. Available at: http://www.eweek.com/networking/hp-green-data-center-vision-offers-eco-friendly-power-cooling-technology.

Carbon Trust (2013). *UK Low Carbon Capabilities Report*. London, Beijing: Carbon Trust.

Conservancy, T. N. (2007). *Partners in Conservation*. Indonesia: The Nature Conservancy. Available at: https://www.nature.or.id/en/publication/annual-report-and-general-conservation-issues/tnci-annual-report-english.pdf.

Corporate Partners (2013). *Conservation International*. Available at: https://www.conservation.org/partners/Pages/alcoa-foundation.aspx.

Environmental Defense Fund (2010). *McDonald's and Environmental Defense Fund Mark 20 Years of Partnerships for Sustainability, Environmental Defense Fund.* Available at: https://www.edf.org/news/mcdonald's-and-environmental-defense-fund-mark-20-years-partnerships-sustainability.

Sarni, W. (2015). "Deflecting the Scarcity Trajectory: Innovation at the Water, Energy, and Food Nexus." *Deliotte Insights*, July. Available at: https://dupress.deloitte.com/dup-us-en/deloitte-review/issue-17/water-energy-food-nexus.html.

Starbucks (2016). *Ethical Sourcing: Coffee.* Available at: https://www.starbucks.com/responsibility/sourcing/coffee.

Tufano, P., Barker, R. and Johnstone-Louis, M. (2016). *In Pursuit of Inclusive Capitalism: Business and Approaches to Systemic Change.* Oxford: The Ford Foundation and Monitor Deloitte. Available at: https://www.sbs.ox.ac.uk/sites/default/files/research-projects/Images/ford-report.pdf.

UN (2014). "The United Nations at a Glance." *United Nations* 89(3): 493–505. Available at: http://www.un.org/en/aboutun/index.shtml.

Werker, E. and Ahmed, F. (2007). "What Do Non-Governmental Organizations Do?" *Economic Perspectives* 22(2).

Part II
The Changing World View

7

Lifeblood of Global Business: Oil and Gas

Oil is both the lifeblood and poison of the global economy. Historically if we think about the control of resources, it confers power to governments and people. Just as those that owned water rights controlled access to irrigation and crops, those that owned food distribution points influence the communities, and those that controlled geographic choke points on trade routes controlled the flow of commerce. In the modern age, oil and gas are no different. Oil and gas provide power and influence to those that control it, and power and influence shapes political agendas, economies, and markets. Oil and gas are not just a resource that provides energy for the world. It is also the most important feedstock for manufactured components that are in demand the world over. Everything from cosmetics to containers, machine parts, fashion, and furniture are all by-products of petroleum. The pervasive nature and the uses of oil and gas comes from the desire for a certain standard of living. It has the potential to influence change in those regions that lack it, and it influences our ability to maintain security or defend against aggression.

With the greening of the world our reliance on oil and gas for energy purposes is going to continue to shrink. Currently, there are no alternative forms of energy that can fully replace this resource for a projected two decades when it will still be the source for over 50 percent of the world's energy needs (BP 2017). With the growth in population expected to grow to 9.8 billion over by 2050 (UN 2017), a majority of that population is demanding western-style living standards with its desire for energy and energy products. Also because of the growth of infrastructure in countries that are seeing the greatest growth, namely, China, Asia, and India, there is high demand for electric power for domestic as well as business use. Demand for crude oil and gas is high and it is expected that there will be continued increase in demand pressure.

The demand pressure places even more burden on access to reserves to meet the requirements for escalating populations and economic growth. Attempts to build reserve depth and resources are evident by efforts to buy futures. The Indian oil companies purchase natural gas from the US and Norwegian interest in the western coast of Africa (PTI 2015). The Chinese are going after assets in the United States, West Africa, and more challenging parts of the world like Venezuela (IDE, no date). These are market positions held to secure national interests in deep resource and reserves. Those countries that can't maintain a stable supply of oil and gas reserves are going to rely on more interdependence and have less independence. It remains the lifeblood of most economic activity and that is unlikely to change in the foreseeable future.

Economic and Geopolitical Impacts

Rising oil prices, both deflationary and inflationary, are a poisonous economic mix. If the price goes too high it depresses the economy while simultaneously increasing inflationary pressure through more spending on oil and less spending on everything else. The weakening demand will cause the price to start falling at which point oil becomes a powerful deflationary force (Warner 2013).

Another characteristic of oil and gas is its connection to geopolitics. Choices have a dynamic, though not perfectly understood, impact on systems. The repercussions of those choices are far reaching as seen by the actions from the Middle East releasing restrictions on production and the immediate dramatic impact on the reduced price per barrel. There is an argument that the action was an intentional strategy designed to combat the rise of "unconventional play" in the United States, declaring energy independence by 2020 (Egan 2016). The backlash and the unintended consequences were that it has actually caused innovation to occur to bring the breakeven point down by almost 40 percent (Crooks 2016). Instead of the Middle East's desired outcome, that US providers were run out of the business, instead the US providers tightened their belts and got smarter about what they were doing. They ended up being fiercer competitors and, coupled with consolidation, exemplified the axiom, "the survival of the fittest." Companies that are the best are the most likely to be strong international competitors in the next ten years. The dynamic system has many undesired consequences that, if not approached with care and consideration, may not achieve the expected objective. Mixing economics and politics is a dangerous cocktail. Rebel forces attacking pipelines in Nigeria are actually controlling the way the Government does business and also impacting market conditions for export. Russia's manipulation of the pipeline into Europe and the manner in which it controlled and restricted flow changed and attempted to influence European Union (EU) decisions and thereby to directly impact the marketplace. Oil and gas introduces a dynamic relationship with the ebbs and flows of prices, technology, extraction of raw materials, and production of refined commodities.

Monetizing the Resources

Wise oil producers are diversifying to control costs. In 1970 the formula was simple, spend an amount of money to punch a hole in the ground and take the same amount of money out of the hole. Today the commodity or sales of oil downstream are highly variable. Therefore, current diversification efforts are in building the petrochemical side of the industry. They are building more durable value into the product lines than they are from the energy side. Those goods are necessary to the marketplace itself and this is a deliberate commercial strategy.

There is an influx of countries going into building infrastructure, water purification plants, energy infrastructure, and creating its own micro market for those support mechanisms. Their goal is to monetize natural resources that they are sitting on and not to rely exclusively on one source for their economy to function. It is challenging for policy planners to think about how to maximize the use of their resources without overproducing and seeking a clear balance between price and consumers alike. To the extent that a consistent predictable smooth demand is created, the global market will find that sweet spot. The clear exception is if there is only one source of income for the country. As an example, Venezuela is a state on the brink of failure because of their reliance on one naturally available resource. Their economy has not moved toward diversity as a natural maturing of their petroleum resources.

It is safe to assume a continued shift away from just pure energy and a movement toward the durable marketplace and high performance petrochemical manufacturing that are designed to take advantage of unconventional innovation to extend the life of oil reservoirs by extracting more feedstock. In contrast, the coal industry has always had one primary driver, energy. There has been limited movement toward development of derivative products like that of the petrochemical industry. As a result coal generally has a bad reputation because of environmental concerns with none of the redeeming qualities as a feedstock for other value added products. There's an interesting play in North America between coal and natural gas where even environmentalists agree that natural gas is substantially better than coal. Natural gas has its own derivative uses other than energy. Large number of US plastics and petrochemical facilities use oil and natural gas derivatives for their products.

Oil Dependent Economies

Countries that rely solely on production for energy purposes must move their demand for oil and gas from energy to value added sources. Developing countries that are just thirsty for energy will drive the energy component of oil and gas. Population growth and a rise in standards of living mean that the demands of a growing middle class will increase to levels never seen before. Demand will stimulate growth in production and distribution of oil and gas products. Several countries are predominantly petroleum economies, namely, Algeria, Brunei, Iraq, Kuwait, Libya, Saudi Arabia, and Venezuela. They depend primarily on oil and gas. Are these countries, with vast oil and gas resources, successful in developing global trade or are they stuck in the curves of natural resources? Part of the answer lies with the leadership and political structure within those countries. It is encouraging to see countries like Saudi Arabia that have built stable economies on the back of oil and gas and are seriously considering diversifying petroleum products. That is forward thinking, they are not reliant on any one subcomponent of the world economy to survive. Dependent countries like Venezuela have gone backwards regarding standards of living and capacity to provide the simple basics for their citizens. China has actually bartered with countries like Venezuela and Angola where the Chinese provide construction and infrastructure development that would likely not have happened had those economies been better managed. Middle Eastern geopolitics are mostly based on religious ideologies with an underlying power struggle between Iran and Saudi Arabia. This undercurrent has a significant influence on how countries are able to take advantage of natural resources. In the end it is the maturity of the leadership that sets the tone for how things work.

At the current level of production Saudi Arabia needs to charge at least $70 per barrel next year to break even in order to balance the budget and support its spending plans, despite reducing the cost to bring it down from $96.60 in 2016, which is still way higher than the twentieth-century break even (Dipaola 2017). Saudi Aramco is the world's largest exporter of crude oil with the world's largest onshore and offshore oil fields (Trotman 2016). They are also the world's most valuable company. Venezuela has the largest share of global oil reserves in the world which is almost 17.5 percent (OPEC 2017). Venezuela's curse right now is not the oil but that their fortunes are closely tied to oil. So closely tied they are that they could not sustain a drop in the price per barrel.

Demand and Supply Equation

Historically there's always been a tension between countries that produce oil and those that consume oil. There was a deficit of flow from where it was sourced to where it was used. Over the past ten years a dramatic flip has developed. Countries with access to their own natural resources but no ability to get them out of the ground and to marketplace had private enterprise, usually international companies, come in to assist. Some of these relationships were quite exploitative. Companies took the oil out and left little profit inside the country. Fortunately, people are smart and learn from experience. Consequently, there has been a rise in companies like the Saudi National Oil Company, Aramco, the gold standard of national oil companies and what is expected is a replication of the standard, outside the inefficiency of many national oil companies. These efforts must be set by a financial objective and not just the political agenda. They must have effective mechanisms to capitalize on the monetizing of precious natural resources for the country. The shift is beginning to be seen and we are observing a switch where companies representing the national interest are being held to higher levels of accountability, efficiency, and capability. The expectation is a transfer of dynamic power in the oil business to those types and processes of natural resources management that are no longer counterproductive.

Saudi Arabian oil companies are generally the source of national income through those big corporations that have bright engineers and good leadership that in the past were pressured by politicians for either social agenda or for other reasons. Today these personal interests are beginning to be exposed. In a digital data driven world, where anyone can find anything about anybody, corruption is set to dissipate slowly. The transparency of the new digital world has created a more efficient and effective operation without the interference of politics. With this "cleaner" field foreign international non-national oil companies should only get better. The number of countries that are reliant on merely domestic production is small and the percentage of domestic consumption is usually three or four times that of domestic production. There is a natural diversification that those national companies have to achieve. These companies are typically politically or socially motivated relying on effective, better use, and more efficient production of energy which usually turns out to be good for the economy.

Interestingly national oil companies are going through a maturing process. They are beginning to take the world stage. Statoil has stakes across the world not just in the Norwegian shelf. Sinopec (China Petroleum & Chemical Corporation) is looking offshore and onshore in South America. They are not confined to their national resources any longer. They are expanding out, and they are stepping into that role confidently.

Business Cycles

The oil and gas industry has gone through a downturn for quite some time and just as Thomas Edison inventing the electric light bulb in 1878 caused a major recession in the oil industry (Laxer 2008), what is the diagnosis for the oil and gas industry? In this current price downturn the answer depends on where you are in the world. US producers and first- and second-tier manufacturers and suppliers are still hurting though they seem to have seen it coming and have innovated around it. The Saudis can only sustain their price for a couple of years more since they have had to rely on capital reserves for four to five years. These countries are willing to give up on the social agenda and get a lot more efficient in the way they use proceeds from the sale of oil. With these downturns come innovation and efficiency gains and different ways of looking at process and operations. It shakes the industry to its foundation and forces a rethink of what the industry looks like. According to Santosh, CEO of Lone Star Group, "I am convinced that the next five years are going to look nothing like the past five years and I have to be strategic in the way I redesign our organisation." He says, "I think the strategies (and) the tactical plans (from the past) are obsolete or irrelevant . . . am convinced we will come out stronger and we will come out more efficient, we will use energy more efficiently, and we will use our most valuable resource our human brains far more effectively."

There are voices that categorize the downturn as part of a normal market cycle, saying that the free market encourages innovation and promotes the development of disruptive technology that will bring out the best in human nature. How do we actually take advantage of the downturn? Practitioners have to take this time to hone their strategies, think about how to maximize performance, and squeeze to ensure they have got the best and brightest talent. They have got to make certain that they are leveraging competitive advantage in a time when others are scrambling for survival. When the economy revives, they will be two steps ahead. Michael Grojean, Principal at Grojean and Associates, Inc., says, that downturn "is the time . . . to do our best development work . . . our deepest thinking."

Sustainable energy sources are under the spotlight and alternative renewable resources are looking more attractive to energy pundits. The utilization of an energy source as a supplement and not a challenge to oil and gas make good sense and is also appropriate for a free market environment. The market competition would force innovation and result in better use of the oil and gas resources. Currently, there's too much money to be made from oil and gas. There is little chance that renewables sources can fund the development necessary to replace mainstream utilisation for power generation. Though they are experiencing market growth in Europe and the United States, renewables are almost always subsidized and built on a carbon footprint or emissions control. These subsidies artificially change the balance of cost thereby making oil or gas production too expensive. Power generation from unconventional sources like solar and wind turbines, etc. are bolstered by production tax credits and are not able to stand alone without government support. However, some companies are putting a lot of time and effort into alternative research and have seen some significant wins.

References

BP (2017). *BP Energy Outlook 2017 Edition*. Available at: https://www.bp.com/content/dam/bp/pdf/energy-economics/energy-outlook-2017/bp-energy-outlook-2017.pdf.

Crooks, E. (2016). "Cost Reductions Help US Shale Oil Industry Pass First Real Test." *Financial Times*, August 28. Available at: https://www.ft.com/content/65ebdd54-6b79-11e6-ae5b-a7cc5dd5a28c.

Dipaola, A. (2017). "Saudi Arabia Leads Gulf Nations in Cutting Break-Even Oil Price." *Bloomberg*, October. Available at: https://www.bloomberg.com/news/articles/2017-10-31/saudi-arabia-leads-gulf-nations-in-cutting-break-even-oil-price.

Egan, M. (2016). "U.S. Energy Independence Looks 'Tantalizingly Close'." *CNN Money*. Available at: http://money.cnn.com/2016/08/09/investing/us-energy-independence-oil-opec/index.html.

IDE (no date). "China in Africa, Institute of Developing Economies." Available at: http://www.ide.go.jp/English/Data/Africa_file/Manualreport/cia_07.html.

Laxer, J. (2008). *Oil*. Edited by J. Springer. Toronto: Groundwood Books.

OPEC (2017). "Share of World Crude Oil reserves," *OPEC Annual Statistical Bulletin*. Available at: http://www.opec.org/opec_web/en/data_graphs/330.htm.

PTI (2015). "Indian Oil Corporation Signs Agreement to Buy 0.7 MT LNG a Year from US." *Economic Times*, May 29. Available at: https://economictimes.indiatimes.com/industry/energy/oil-gas/indian-oil-corporation-signs-agreement-to-buy-0-7-mt-lng-a-year-from-us/articleshow/47475484.cms.

Trotman, A. (2016). "Saudi Arabia Confirms Scheme to List Aramco, World's Largest Oil Producer." *The Telegraph*, January 8. Available at: http://www.telegraph.co.uk/finance/newsbysector/energy/oilandgas/12087397/Saudi-Arabia-looks-at-listing-worlds-largest-oil-producer.html.

UN (2017). "World Population Projected to Reach 9.8 Billion in 2050, and 11.2 Billion in 2100." *United Nations Department of Economic and Social Affairs*. Available at: https://www.un.org/development/desa/en/news/population/world-population-prospects-2017.html.

Warner, J. (2013). "Oil is Both the Lifeblood and the Poison of the Global Economy." *The Telegraph*, November 21. Available at: http://www.telegraph.co.uk/finance/oilprices/10465340/Oil-is-both-the-lifeblood-and-the-poison-of-the-global-economy.html.

8

Emerging Economies as Growth Drivers

The fortunes of emerging economies and developed economies are interlocked. One cannot function well without the other. Together they move the wheels of the global economy. The role of emerging markets is changing in the twenty-first century from the traditional provider of low-cost, labor-intensive goods to a growth engine of the global world. These emerging economies are growing at double the rate of advanced economies because of technology and global connectivity. Traditionally they have been big exporters of commodities and raw materials to the rest of the world. The export of commodities has contributed significantly to the development of industrial and physical infrastructure in many countries around the world. However, emerging markets are also lucrative markets and an important source of growth for many international companies as they export their products or increase their presence in these markets by opening subsidiaries or through joint venture mechanisms. Today these markets are coming into their own, moving from sole source exporters feeding the world's growth to becoming increasingly significant normative economic members of the global family.

The Changing Role of Emerging Markets

Traditionally, emerging economies have been an important base for sourcing labor-intensive goods and services. Many ready-to-wear garments found in malls and fashion brand stores are made in emerging markets. An inquiry about service or a product from a company may well be sourced to a call center somewhere in one of these markets. However, in recent years, they are playing a more significant role. This relates to their role as suppliers of capital, talent, and innovation. These factors contribute in a major way to enhance the competitiveness of companies around the world. Emerging economies' contribution toward the growth of the global economy is now higher than the contribution of the advanced economies. The advanced economies are growing at approximately 2 percent per annum whereas emerging ones are growing at about 4.5 percent per annum (World Bank 2016). This means that these markets are playing a significant role in the context of the global economy. The United Nations Conference on Trade and Development (UNCTAD) says that the developing and emerging global economy's global foreign direct investment share increased from 29 percent in 2007 to 52 percent in 2013 (IBS 2015). The developing economy's share in merchandise export rose to 45 percent in 2013, up from 34 percent in 2004 (IBS 2015). In 2007 all of the top 20 companies came from developed economies with nine companies from the United States, ten from Europe, and one from Japan. In a span of six years the situation changed dramatically, and in 2013, seven of the top 20 came from emerging markets with five companies coming from China and one each from Brazil and Russia (IBS 2015).

Christine Lagarde, the Managing Director of the International Monetary Fund (IMF) has highlighted the importance of emerging markets in everyday life:

> Let us consider all the possible connections with emerging markets in the first 30 minutes of a day in a student's life in University. It's 7:00 am and the alarm goes off on your Chinese-made smartphone. On the way to the shower you send a WhatsApp message to your friend. WhatsApp, of course, was co-founded by a Ukrainian computer engineer. A few minutes later your roommate has just awaken and with the number of international graduate students attending foreign universities there is a good chance they may be facetiming with relatives in India. At 7:15 am you are facing a really tough choice between strong coffee from Kenya and a milder variety out of Colombia. You switch on your Bluetooth speaker, made in Malaysia, to listen to the news. Overnight the global stock markets were rattled by the latest Chinese economic data, which has put a dent in your mom's savings plan and you worry about Spring Break in Mexico. Luckily, as you head out to a field trip in a Zip Car made in Korea, you realize that low oil demand and strong supply from emerging markets have also brought down gas prices! As you contemplate these first minutes of your day, you realize that the centre of economic gravity has been slowly shifting. The United States may still be the most important economy in the world, but New York, Chicago, and L.A. have gotten company, from Beijing to Brasilia, from Moscow to Mumbai, and from Jakarta to Johannesburg. (IMF 2016)

Attributes

Several attributes make emerging markets attractive to international business. First, there is a significant market opportunity both for products and services. This is a combination of the young demographics in many emerging economies and the rising purchasing power of the consuming classes. Then there's a whole class of highly aspirational customers who are interested in buying products and services which will enhance their quality of life and who see the consumption of such products as the basis for their happiness and satisfaction.

Another interesting attribute of emerging markets is entrepreneurial energy. When you travel through these countries, you see that there is a strong surge in entrepreneurship. In countries like China and India, there are millions of micro and small businesses that are contributing to the local economy and creating employment opportunities for the unskilled, semi-skilled, and skilled workforce. This is an example of what is sometimes called the "hidden workforce," which includes the street vendors, delivery services, housewives, and taxi drivers etc. that represent almost three billion workers around the world. Many of them are linked seamlessly to medium and large businesses providing some vital industrial products and services. This is an attractive trend in these economies, and it is definitely a method by which the process of industrialization and the phenomenon of market-based economies spreading throughout the country and even going to the smaller towns.

The third attribute of the emerging market is a massive growth in the education sector. The number of technology graduates coming out of China, India, and Brazil far exceeds the number of technical graduates coming from several developed countries. These technology graduates are the key to the success and the increasing dominance of companies in the technology and service sectors. In the past, low-cost production was attributed to the attractiveness of these economies. However, there has been a certain erosion of that because wages have been increasing.

Changing Business Models

In the western world, there has been a respectable improvement in productivity. A consequence of this is that many western companies are now undertaking production domestically rather than going to an emerging market or outsourcing their production. In the pharmaceutical sector, for example, a fascinating model is evolving. It is a combination of low-cost model combined with a highly skilled pool of talent that makes emerging economies attractive for research and development. For example, Bangalore in India hosts several hundred pharmaceutical companies regarding their research and development activities. In addition to the trends discussed earlier, some of the other things that make emerging economies very attractive are the rapid urbanization and growth of public infrastructure taking place in these countries.

That offers great opportunities for organizations or companies involved in environmental technologies, provision of water, power, communication, transport, and security. New opportunities are arising out of modernization and the extension of the industrial economy and agricultural economy of global markets. There is an increase in demand for professional services. In short, there are many different attributes which make emerging markets very attractive.

We can learn lessons from successful companies as well as from many businesses that failed to capitalize on the attractiveness of these developing markets. First, western organizations have to be cautious. They must follow a learning approach rather than an approach in which they choose the predetermined solution. Each emerging market is a different type of market. It is hard to standardize the political and process solutions, product solutions, or service solutions across all emerging economies. There are many local, cultural factors, and local preferences tend to differ. The learning-oriented approach is a must for organizations from the western world if they want to explore and seek benefits from the opportunities that exist in these developing economies. Second, there is a real need for organizations to educate those based in the company's headquarters. Traditionally, the headquarter model of western companies has been such that they tend to make decisions based on familiarity and comfort. Often there may be major knowledge gaps at the level of the top decision makers about emerging markets. It is important that the strategic decision makers leave their headquarters and visit emerging markets to see what is happening at the ground level and then to act at the country market level, making appropriate decisions aligned with the demands of local consumers.

Building relationships is crucial to engaging with emerging economies. There is a need to develop relationships with multiple stakeholders in governments because they dominate policy media, owners of the distribution channels, and more. A hybrid management team comprised of locals and expatriates would be very helpful in this regard. Utilizing local resources regarding capital, talent, raw materials, and local entrepreneurs not only builds relationships but strengthens the market.

There is a definite shortage of talent in emerging economies, particularly those skilled at the managerial and executive levels. Companies need to have a strong, attractive employee value proposition that enables them to attract the best talent. Therefore, foreign companies must ensure that they have taken precautionary measures to protect their intellectual property. Fundamentally, foreign companies must be able to interlock their operations in the developed and developing countries to exploit the competitive advantages that exist.

Interlocking of Developed and Emerging Economies

Technology transfer between developed and emerging markets is a challenging issue. Intellectual property also becomes a big issue. Licensing is still the preferred and most frequently used mechanism for transferring technology. However, many large international companies have located their own research and development centers in local markets to develop products to match local tastes and preferences. GE, for instance, has been following an interesting approach called reverse innovation. They have been developing new products in these markets and then marketing the products globally. Companies operating like this will have to be careful regarding how they transfer technology to protect their intellectual property.

As to whether emerging economies will dominate globalization, there are several answers. If we focus on their contribution to the growth of the global economy, then the answer is, yes. However, this reply is based purely on statistics. It will not be easy for any one country to dominate the market globally because there have been accelerated developments not just in the emerging markets but also in advanced economies. The corresponding bargaining power of these new markets has been improving significantly. Observation indicates a levelling off of the relationships between the advanced economies and developing markets. The fortunes of developed countries and emerging economies are interlocked. One cannot grow without the other, and together they move the wheels of the world's economy. It is unlikely that one country will dominate as the world is developing stronger relationships in which all markets can win.

Advanced economies have to recognize emerging ones as important partners in the larger interests of the global society. Together they should forge a common mission, to improve the quality of life on the planet earth. Both players must sit at the same table and agree on ways to further common goals. This involves lowering tariffs and non-tariff barriers to boost the exchange of goods, services, knowledge, and talent across borders. It is time to strengthen global institutions by adopting internationally acceptable mechanisms to promote trade among nations.

Companies, for their part, must recognize the virtues of diversity and develop seamless operations by interlocking value chain and business models across advanced economies and emerging markets. This is an important role for political leaders as well as corporate leaders in advanced countries. They must have a purpose which is wider than a pure self-interest or the need to make profit. They should think about how they can transform the nature of business relationships between advanced economies and emerging ones. How can they transform the life of the people in these markets and contribute toward lessening inequalities? How can they build alliances such as public-private partnerships. There is a lot to be done by both political leaders and corporate leaders from developed countries and a significant opportunity for them to play a primary role in emerging economies.

Inequality and Poverty

Here is the paradox. There is a noticeable increase in the income in certain socioeconomic groups of people and they tend to benefit more from the current phase of globalization. In many emerging markets there is evidence that suggests inequality is growing. That could be because of the uneven growth of industrial and social infrastructure in these countries. A handful of the major cities tends to become the concentrated centers for industrialization. These more affluent groups are inclined to grab major chunks of investment within the social infrastructure which, combined with their entrepreneurial ambition and highly educated investors, tend to accumulate greater benefit. If we look at the lower end of the societal spectrum, the poor socioeconomic classes, we find they are not getting the same level of benefit from globalization, which contributes to increased inequality. There are also examples of a strong positive impact on society with regards to poverty reduction. As per the World Bank publication of March 28, 2017, China has lifted 800 million people out of poverty since initiating its reforms in 1978 (World Bank 2017).

Another factor is the behavior of the political classes. The political classes still encourage a lot of crony capitalism. Their system of political patronage, even though there are efforts to reduce and eliminate the corruption, still remains in place. There is still significant corruption in many emerging economies, and this creates a distinct social imbalance. There are some societies in which select people have more privileges because of their closeness to the political leadership in contrast to others who may not be affiliated with the political class. This is a massive contributor to inequality.

The final reason that inequalities are growing is the result of social policy. There is a greater degree of focus on industrialization and numerous privileges and incentives for the investors and industrialists, often at the cost of reducing social program budgets. Numerous economists have speculated that this spells disaster for emerging markets because it creates a wider social and economic divide between classes in these economies. A disturbing example is the health standards in some of these markets where governments do not have the money to spend on healthcare, resulting in heavy health-related economic costs from diseases that tend to inflict lower income classes.

Despite a variety of issues being faced by emerging economies, they are contributing immensely to the global economy and have succeeded in pulling millions of people out of poverty. The world economy will depend on these developing markets in the twenty-first century for growth.

References

IBS (2015). *Importance of Emerging Markets in today's world, IBS India*. Available at: https://www.linkedin.com/pulse/importance-emerging-markets-todays-world-hina-deo.

IMF (2016). "The Role of Emerging Markets in a New Global Partnership for Growth by IMF Managing Director Christine Lagarde." International Monetary Fund. Available at: https://www.imf.org/en/News/Articles/2015/09/28/04/53/sp020416.

World Bank (2016). *The World Bank DataBank, Data Bank*. Available at: http://databank.worldbank.org/data/home.aspx.

World Bank (2017). *China Overview*. Available at: http://www.worldbank.org/en/country/china/overview.

9

China's Re-emergence as a Global Power

Over the past five decades China's unprecedented rise is one of the rare economic success stories of a country opening up its economy to world markets. China initiated market reforms in 1978 with a major shift to a market-based economy from a centrally planned economy. The move resulted in an unprecedented economic growth and social impact. The gross domestic product (GDP) growth has averaged close to double digits for most of the time since then, and created a major economy at the fastest pace in history. It has made a major contribution to global growth since the financial crisis of 2008. In 2015, China was ranked number one in terms of GDP and purchasing power parity (PPP) at $19.8 trillion, followed by the United States at $18 trillion (World Bank 2017).

Another major achievement of China has been the lifting of more than 800 million people out of poverty (World Bank 2017). It also succeeded in meeting all the Millennium Development Goals (MDG) by 2015. The MDGs are eight goals with measurable targets and clear deadlines for improving the lives of the world's poorest people. To meet these goals and eradicate poverty, leaders of 189 countries signed the historic millennium declaration at the United Nations Millennium Summit in 2000 (UN 2000). China has now become the second largest world economy with a population of 1.3 billion (UN 2017). However, it still remains a developing country because its per capita income is much lower than that of developed countries. If its growth rate can be sustained, through methods such as major policy adjustments, China—already moving from low income into middle income—will be poised to make the difficult transition to high income.

History

China is large. It has a land mass of 9.6 million square kilometers with borders touching Afghanistan, Bhutan, Hong Kong, India, Kazakhstan, Kyrgyzstan,

Laos, Macau, Mongolia, Nepal, Pakistan, North Korea, Tajikistan, Vietnam, and Russia (Worldatlas 2017).

China has the longest continually recorded history in the pre-modern world. There was a sharp contrast between China's pre-imperial era before 220 BC and its imperial era after that. The Chinese Empire successfully built a mixed economy of commerce, farming, handicrafts, and pastoralism. It promoted science and technology as well as literature and art. This was known as "a hundred flowers blossoming" (*baijia zhengming*, literally "a grand song contest with one hundred contenders"). During 206 BC– 24 AD, it converted its political and economic systems into a package of an imperial bureaucracy under a fiscal state and economy under agricultural dominance which caused a change in the trajectory of growth and development, and weakened Feudalism for rest of the imperial period till 1800 (Deng, no date).

The Historical Chinese Markets and the Market Economy

The economy that developed in pre-modern China was driven by high-yield agriculture that produced a constant surplus. Production was taxed and the proceeds invested inside the economy. By the end of the Qing (1912), one-third of their agricultural output was surplus and became the foundation of the development of other sectors of the economy (Deng, no date). Monetization in China coincided with the Empire itself. Coins were mass produced by state mints and in the period from 960 to 1368 AD. cloth and paper were also used as currency on a large scale because of the lack of metals (Deng, no date). From the fifteenth to nineteenth centuries China imported foreign silver, with almost one-third of the total of silver output from the New World landing in China. It became the standard of their economy. This practice, once the market was saturated with foreign silver, caused price revolutions that led to the devaluation of the currency (Deng, no date).

China has a long history of strong market activity, but it lacked the tradition of a merchant class. The feudal aristocracy representing the talented and wealthy "officialdom" (bureaucracy) resulted in social mobility based on position (privileged class) rather than on achievement or performance. The Chinese markets were multi-layered. At the grassroots they were local and decentralized but the top level, the market highly structured and dominated by state-controlled commodities like salt, iron and steel, and wine. Foreign trade was the monopoly of the state (Deng, no date). By the early nineteenth century China was manufacturing almost one-third of the world capacity and was the single largest supplier of ceramics and silk. It sold paper, stationary, and cooking pots in the Asian markets. It used its trade to obtain silver in order to play a central role in the currency system (Deng, no date).

Science and Technology

China was one of the main centers for developing new technologies and scientific discoveries in the pre-modern world. It was leading the world in science and technology in the period between the tenth and fifteenth centuries. The focus of their scientific and technological discoveries included material production, transport, weaponry, and medicine. Such discoveries, though significant, resulted in incremental economic improvement based on a trial-and-error methodology. The lack of strategic cohesiveness limited development and produced diminishing returns. Although a leader in science and technology at one time, China could not convert their innovation into long-term gains or a primary world leadership role (Deng, no date).

Economic Progress

Two hundred years ago the Chinese economy was the largest in the world. China's GDP at that time was twice that of the second largest economy (India), six times the size of Britain, and 20 times the size of United States. The per capita GDP of China reached 84 percent of the global average in the year 1820, which went down to 60 percent by 1870, and 24 percent in 1980. China's economic decline in the latter half of the nineteenth century was caused by the devastation of agricultural lands after the Opium War in the period 1839 to 1842 and the Taiping Rebellion from 1850 to 1864. Western nations gained wealth with the Industrial Revolution in the nineteenth century while China lost ground economically. In late 1970s Deng Xiaoping started his implementation of market-based reforms which triggered the modernization of China and it has now re-emerged as an economic superpower in the global arena (Globalist 2014).

The rapid growth of past decades has created challenges too. It created quite a few billionaires in the country but economic inequality has risen. The rapid urbanization of the country, due to the migration of labor, has created challenges around environmental sustainability. An ageing population is creating demographic pressure. The thirteenth five-year plan is focused on the quality of growth with a lower planned rate of growth. Despite this, it is likely that the country's GDP will have doubled in the decade ending in 2020. The plan moves the focus toward addressing social issues in access to education, healthcare, reduction in pollution, increase in energy efficiency, and social protection (CCCPC 2016).

Balance of Trade

The Chinese economy is the largest exporter in the world with $2.37 trillion exports against imports of $1.27 trillion creating a positive trade balance of $1.1 trillion (2015), which is more than the GDP of most developing countries. The GDP for the same period was $11 trillion and GDP per capita of $14,500 (WTO 2017). The per capita GDP is especially useful when comparing one country to another because it shows the relative performance of the countries. A rise in per capita GDP signals growth in the economy and tends to reflect an increase in productivity. The vast differences in per capita GDP are exemplified by comparisons between developed and developing economies. For example, at $153 million, Qatar had the highest 2016 worker output in the world when adjusted for PPP, a measure that pegs each nation's currency to the US dollar for comparative purposes. By contrast, Ethiopia, which sits toward the bottom of the global scale, held a per capita GDP of $72 million in 2016 (World Bank 2017).

Chinese imports increased by 5.7 percent in the five-year period from 2010 to 2015 with exports growing from $1.75 trillion to $2.37 trillion. The top importers of goods from China are United States, Hong Kong, Japan, Germany, and South Korea. The top import locations for China are South Korea, United States, Japan, Germany, and other Asian countries. In the year 2016, the top exports from China were computers ($136 billion), broadcasting equipment ($115 billion), telephones ($84.3 billion), integrated circuits ($54.8 billion), and light fixtures ($29.7 billion). Its top imports in 2016 were integrated circuits ($128 billion), crude petroleum ($116 billion), gold ($62.6 billion), iron ore ($58 billion), and automobiles ($44 billion) (OECD 2015; OEC 2017).

Factory of the World

In the last half a century, China has transformed itself by manufacturing goods and selling them to the rest of the world and in the process it changed the global economy. In 1990, China produced less than 3 percent of global manufacturing output by value. Their output has increased to 25 percent. China produces about 80 percent of the world's air-conditioners, 70 percent of its mobile phones, and 60 percent of its shoes. China has followed the "Asian Tigers," South Korea and Taiwan, in the manufacturing of inexpensive products. It was expected that, after its phenomenal growth and rising wages, it would pass the accessible product baton to other countries of the world, however it seems China has not conceded its position, and is still holding on to the low-cost manufacturing monopoly. There are signs, however, that some of the low-end manufacturing has moved to countries like Indonesia, Vietnam, and Cambodia with China changing its focus to higher-value addition work (Economist 2015).

The World Bank highlighted an interesting point about China. The percentage of imported components in China's total exports has gone down from 60 percent in the mid-1990s to around 35 percent today (Economist 2015). This has been possible because of the development of local efficient supply chains which others cannot replicate. The Government's Made in China 2025 strategy cites automation as the means to increase productivity and to offset the effect of increasing wages. To support business with infrastructure improvement, the Government has plans to build ten airports a year until 2020. Chinese manufacturing is also backed by their large population which represents a huge consumer base and demand (Economist 2015).

The largest manufacturing economy of the world is also the most competitive nation in the world. The economy, which was driven initially by its ability to deliver low-cost labor and materials, is already making moves to create other competitive drivers like infrastructure, favorable policies, a large population as a consumer base, and a well-established supplier network. It is making significant progress in its capabilities, moving from manufacturing low-cost goods to more advanced value-added products.

Key Factors in China's Success

China has accomplished a remarkable feat in transforming itself from one of the world's poorest countries to the second largest economy in just 30 years. There have been several factors accounting for this success. China's economic growth can be seen as largely labor-intensive, with high levels of fixed capital investment. Key factors for growth in GDP have been an increase in total factor productivity (TFP, which is productivity of labor and capital) and fixed asset investments. Since 1979, the increase in TFP has contributed almost 40 percent of GDP growth. The initial bounce in productivity came from urbanization with the movement of people from sluggish rural economies to more efficient urban jobs. In addition, the shifting of resources from the public sector to the private contributed almost 8 percent of the growth in China's GDP. In addition the mass movement of workers from state-owned firms to the private sector was another factor that improved productivity. The contribution of investments in fixed assets also contributed another 40 percent of growth in GDP in the same period. In the mid- to late nineties when the economy was on the path to growth it received another push from foreign direct investment and joint ventures with developed countries.

Relationships with the rest of the world improved as growth in exports kept fueling the economy (Yeuh 2013).

China now has a lower rate of growth planned which is still, however, substantially higher than that of the developed world. To continue its growth in coming decades, China will have to move from reliance on low-cost exports to expand its local consumer demand. It will require a continuation of reforms and further enhancement to unleash the spending power of Chinese consumers and build a more balanced economy. The process will involve the boosting of demand through consumption, investment, and government spending. It will require technological developments, human capital improvements, legal reforms, and clarity on the role of the state, re-balancing the economy with domestic demand growing at a rate higher than the exports, and building the services sector.

The role of the state has been critical in the growth of China, and it will remain so along with its legal system. The market efficiency of China may improve with actions being taken to provide a level playing field for foreign as well as domestic private firms. The right steps at this stage will help it to avoid the "middle-income country trap," and enable continued growth. For China to realize its potential as an economic superpower requires reforms of both the microeconomic drivers of productivity as well as the significant transformation of the structure of its economy.

References

CCCPC (2016). *The 13th Five-Year Plan for Economic and Social Development of the People's Republic Of China (2016–2020)*. Beijing. Available at: http://en.ndrc.gov.cn/news release/201612/P020161207645765233498.pdf.

Deng, K. (no date). "Economic History of Premodern China (from 221 BC to c. 1800 AD)." *Economic History Association*. Available at: https://eh.net/encyclopedia/economic-history-of-premodern-china-from-221-bc-to-c-1800-ad/.

Economist (2015). "Global Manufacturing Made in China?" *The Economist*, March. Available at: https://www.economist.com/news/leaders/21646204-asias-dominance-manufacturing-will-endure-will-make-development-harder-others-made.

Globalist, T. (2014). "12 Facts on China's Economic History China's Boom Restores the Country's Former Global Economic Preeminence." *The Globalist*. Available at: https://www.theglobalist.com/12-facts-on-chinas-economic-history/.

OEC (2017). "China." *OEC*. Available at: https://atlas.media.mit.edu/en/profile/country/chn/.

OECD (2015). "OECD Data China, People's Republic of." *OECD*. Available at: https://data.oecd.org/china-people-s-republic-of.htm.

UN (2000). *Millennium Summit (6–8 September 2000). Millennium declaration, UN*. Available at: http://www.un.org/en/events/pastevents/millennium_summit.shtml.

UN (2017). *Population, United Nations*. Available at: http://www.un.org/en/sections/issues-depth/population/index.html.

World Bank (2017). *China Overview*. Available at: http://www.worldbank.org/en/country/china/overview.

Worldatlas (2017). "Geography Statistics Of China." *Worldatlas*. Available at: http://www.worldatlas.com/webimage/countrys/asia/china/cnlandst.htm.

WTO (2017). *World Trade Statistical Review*. Available at: https://www.wto.org/english/res_e/statis_e/wts2016_e/wts2016_e.pdf.

Yeuh, L. (2013). *China's Growth The Making of an Economic Superpower*. Oxford: Oxford University Press.

10

The Knowledge Barons of India

India's economic journey has seen many ups and downs since 3,500 BCE. The country accounted for a quarter of global industrial output in the 1700s but dropped down to 2 percent by the mid-1900s (Clingingsmith and Williamson 2005). Since its independence in 1947, it has had a slow growth rate which experienced a dramatic turn with the liberalization of the economy in the 1990s. It has become the third largest economy in terms of gross domestic product (GDP) in purchasing power parity (PPP) (WB 2017). With 900 million mobile phone users, it has the second largest English-speaking population after the United States (NASSCOM 2015). India has successfully built its knowledge-based industry with software exports being its primary product. Of late the Government has taken aggressive steps to move toward a cashless transaction society by driving digitization. It also made the tough decision to de-monetize the currency in an attempt to eradicate corruption and provide an alternate platform for electronic payments. The recent sector-wide policy intervention by the Government, intended to drive economic growth, may create a completely new growth story in the future. Its large consumer base is an attractive market, and demographic diversity is a competitive advantage. Investments in infrastructure and digital business are being supported by the Government's online e-governance platform. India is the fastest growing emerging economy in the world with a population of 1.3 billion people and an unemployment rate of 4.5 percent in September of 2017 (UN 2017; BSE 2017). The main components of their $2 trillion GDP are services, industry, and agriculture (Bakshi 2016). India is poised to be one of the next economic giants.

History

The history of India began with the dawn of the Indus Valley civilization which flourished from 3500 BCE to 1800 BCE. The Indus civilization's economy depended significantly on trade, which was facilitated by advances in transport. Its citizens were involved in agriculture, keeping domesticated animals, they made sharp tools and weapons from copper, bronze, and tin, and traded in terracotta pots, beads, gold and silver, coloured gemstones such as turquoise and lapis lazuli, metals, flints, seashells, and pearls. They used ships to reach Mesopotamia where they sold gold, copper, and jewellery (Trautmann 2015).

Around 600 BCE, India minted punch-marked coins. For almost 1500 years, India produced classical civilizations. It was a very rich and prosperous country, being the largest economy around the seventeenth century CE. After that the economic fortunes of India declined rapidly during the European colonization. When the British started their expansion in 1700, India accounted for one-quarter of global industrial production, compared to the United Kingdom's 11 percent. However, by 1947, India accounted for less than 2 percent of global wealth (Malone M. David, Mohan, and Raghavan 2015). After gaining independence from Great Britain, from 1947 to 1979 the economy grew at an average rate of about 3.1 percent a year in constant prices. The rate of growth improved in the 1980s. From FY 1980 to FY 1989, the economy grew at an annual rate of 5.5 percent (OECD 2015).

During the late 1980s, India relied increasingly on borrowing from foreign sources. This trend led to a balance of payments crisis in 1990 which triggered economic liberalization. Since then the economy has grown considerably with GDP rising at the rate of 6–8 percent per annum. GDP has increased from $267.52 billion (USD) in 1992 to more than $2.0 trillion. The gains made in 25 years after the liberalization of the economy have been outstanding. A look back at the numbers 25 years ago reveals that the GDP growth rate has changed from −1.4 percent to 7.5 percent, those living below the poverty line has decreased from 45 percent to 22 percent, forex reserves have increased from $9.2 billion to $355 billion, exports increased from $19 billion to $355 billion, imports increased from $9.2 billion to $262 billion, and the literacy rate has improved from 52 percent to 74 percent (Bakshi 2016).

Changing Scenario

The past decade has seen a phenomenal coagulation of elements in India that have led to their emergence as a premier economy on the world stage. The momentum of the twenty-first century has India on a perfect trajectory. Prime Minister, Narendra Modi, has initiated aggressive internal and external policies that have the potential to change Indian culture and firmly move India to becoming the strongest economy on earth. Though this journey has just started, there are already impressive initiatives that are indicators of change, such as several government-driven initiatives focusing on infrastructure. India is poised to realize its demographic dividend. It has the largest population of young people across the globe and also has the ability to train them to produce meaningful output.

Space

India has made considerable progress in science and technology. India's Mars orbiter mission to send a vehicle into orbit around the red planet cost only $74 million, which is actually less than the $100 million it cost to make the Hollywood blockbuster movie, "Gravity" (Thornhill and Zolfagharifard 2014). India has been successful in launching rockets into space at a very low cost. In February of 2017, India's space agency successfully launched a record breaking 104 satellites into orbit on board a single rocket. The previous record was 37 satellites by Russia in 2014 (Safi 2017).

Rail and Road

India has the third largest railway network in the world with 12,000 trains which carry about 20 million passengers every day. Also, there are 7,400 commercial trains which carry three million tons of freight every day and accounts for 15 percent of public transport and 30 percent of freight. The rail system employs 1.4 million people and is the fifth largest employer in the world (Singh 2015). One of the initiatives in place is the modernization of the rail system.

Road infrastructure has characteristically built a couple of kilometers of road a day. In the past three years, significant changes have increased construction by tenfold. There are plans to expand construction of networks of interstate highways. The total investment target for road development over the next three years is $100 billion (Chitnis 2017).

Waterways

A significant amount of work is being done in the development of ports and coastal areas. In rural areas, rivers which are being used for water are being developed to create waterways. There are hundreds of waterways that could be used for transportation and trade. The planned investment to develop these is running into several billion dollars.

Housing

One big ticket item is addressing the Indian housing problem. The plan is to create housing opportunity for every Indian citizen by 2022. The Government plans to give grants directly to households for the rehabilitation of slum housing, make loans available to the poor at discounted rates, and provide additional subsidies. The idea is to ensure that every person in the country, even those on low or no incomes, has access to affordable housing by the target date (2022) (Deloitte 2016). This significant challenge would also create lots of economic opportunities in addition to creating meaningful domestic employment.

Made in India

The manufacturing initiative typically labelled "Made in India" has two elements: "Made in India for India" and "Made in India for the Globe." Made in India has multiple sectors identified as opportunities and specific targets. For example, some higher level sectors like aerospace, automobile, chemical, food processing, construction equipment, technology and electronics, pharmaceuticals, and textiles have been identified by the government for development.

Infrastructure

There is also activity underway to make it easier to do business in India, including efforts to attract investors, especially foreign direct investment. There are specific approval processes and policies already created to make India more conducive to commerce. There is a significant effort to build new cities and enhance the existing ones. The focus is on smart cities through rejuvenation and modernization by putting emphasis on infrastructure. Amenities like adequate water supply, electricity, sanitation, waste management, digitization, public transport, safety, and education are being targeted. A budget of several billion has been reserved to address other infrastructure projects like power generation, capacity, and transmission. The goal is to ensure that India delivers power stability to all households, industry, commercial business, and agriculture.

Digital India

One of the most important changes taking place in India is the foundation, focus, and future of Digital India. Digital India is building the capability across every sector; that is, communication, information technology, rural and urban development, human resources, family, health, welfare, infrastructure, manufacturing, and services. The goal is to have a common delivery platform driving toward a self-reliant economy. Broadly there are three key areas of emphasis. First, the creation of infrastructure and digital businesses which services every citizen. Second, the creation of an on-demand access to government and services. Finally, to empower the people of India to use technology as a competitive advantage globally. This starts with the idea of connecting every part of India, with its thousands of villages in the remotest parts of India, to digital broadband. It also intends to create access to the public network through digital connectivity. That includes focus on creating public programmatic access ensuring that government is accessible through an "e-governance" route. E-governance will be accessible from a quarter of a million planned internet sites expanding from the 135,000 in existence today. Village connectivity will require almost a $5 billion investment. India is fully invested in fiber optic networks which is facilitating government access to everyone. The objective is to create half a million jobs in rural areas by using training programs driven by technology and connectivity all over the country (Deloitte 2015).

The plan is to connect large parts of India through the Wi-Fi network with a secured email system and making the government infrastructure available electronically. These networks have allowed India to leapfrog to other deliverables such as financial services. Some of the other major initiatives toward digitization of the country are Aadhaar Card and Mobile. India launched a unique digital identification program for all its citizens called Aadhaar which now covers almost a billion people. The country is planning to use the reach of mobile phones for connectivity and ease of transactions with 900 million users, of which nearly 40 percent (350 million) are in rural areas (NASSCOM 2015). By using a unique identifier combined with connective mobility, this establishes an infrastructure that allows people to receive authentication for individual transactions immediately. As an example, the entire public subsidy system used to transfer money through the banking system. In that system a simple public to private transfer of capital could take months. Today the identical transaction moving through Aadhaar takes a fraction of a second. In addition the Government saves a significant amount of money. In one program providing subsidy for cooking gas, transferring the funds through the digital system saved several hundred million dollars in one year. Just through digital applications to other government programs like education, healthcare, and pension funds, will bring about efficiencies and minimize process time thereby saving significant capital.

Another basic advantage of this unique identification system is that money goes to the right person with no leakage and moves at phenomenal speeds. This infrastructure is then taken to the next level, facilitating personal identification through online registration with India's public systems thereby eliminating the need for carrying copies of various documents for completing the transaction. A simple bank transfer in the past required a trip to a bank, completion of request forms, the writing of a check, time spent in the queue, numerous other institutional steps, and then a delay of a week before the money was received. Today, a mobile phone enables authentication by putting your finger on the phone's biometric scanner, which can be done from anywhere in the country or the world, and the money appears in less than three seconds. To maintain even better security there's a second authentication method connected to the individual user who retains enough control to monitor the transaction.

The most recent initiative is the National Payments Corporation of India which is akin to a central bank. This body enables account to account transactions through mobile devices. India has the world's highest penetration of mobile devices in terms of growth percentage and is doing significant work providing the last mile connectivity. However, it has one more noteworthy advantage. India has a strong emerging young workforce born within the last 20 years who have been exposed to the digital way of working their entire life. They were born into the digital age. This is beginning a huge shift in the way India operates in comparison to today's workforce. The future of India is going to be fully digital in every aspect.

The Future

People who look at India are starting to see India as a consumer market also. It has a large population with huge consumption demands. India has built up almost $400 billion in foreign-exchange reserves (Sircar and Nag 2017). It is the world's second-largest English speaking country next to the United States. It is a business hub and interacts with people from around the world. It exports to 90 countries with an approximate value of almost $100 billion with software exports being a primary product (NASSCOM 2015).

India has identified ten sectors as being key for partnerships with numerous companies and countries visiting India. Indian businesses are traveling the world and there is clear direction in government policy regarding ways of doing business, trade and the environment, sensible ways of transacting, and the attraction of foreign direct investments. India has become a global player that can participate and build capacity and capability to manufacture across those ten sectors in the Indian market. Henry Kissinger in his latest book, *World Order*, said, "In any scenario, India will be a crucial element for future order in this century because of its resources, geography, leadership and ideology." India stands on the global stage (Kissinger 2015).

The potential to derail this juggernaut, other than the deleterious effect of the interconnected nature of the world's economic system, might be the geopolitics of the country. If the Government changes and ideological drivers change, or if political will fails to follow through on emerging initiatives, or the need for simplification of the tax regime never happens, then there may be different outcomes.

References

Bakshi, I. (2016). "25 Years of Reform." *Business Standard.*

BSE (2017). *Unemployment Rate in India, A collaborative effort of BSE & CMIE.* Available at: https://unemploymentinindia.cmie.com/.

Chitnis, P. (2017). "Indian Roads A $100-Billion Opportunity Over Next Three Years." *Bloomberg.* Available at: https://www.bloombergquint.com/business/2017/07/18/india-to-spend-nearly-rs-7-lakh-crore-on-roads-over-next-three-years-nomura.

Clingingsmith, D. and Williamson, J. G. (2005). "India's Deindustrialization in the 18th and 19th Centuries." Cambridge MA: Harvard University Press.

Deliotte (2015). *Digital India: Unleashing Prosperity.* Available at: https://www2.deloitte.com/content/dam/Deloitte/in/Documents/technology-media-telecommunications/in-tmt-tele-tech-2015-noexp.pdf.

Deloitte (2016). *Mainstreaming Affordable Housing in India Moving towards Housing for All by 2022.* Available at: https://www2.deloitte.com/content/dam/Deloitte/in/Documents/public-sector/in-ps-affordable-housing-noexp.pdf.

Kissinger, H. (2015). *World Order.* USA: Penguin Random House.

Malone M. David, Mohan, C. R., and Raghavan, S. (2015). "A New Set of Views on Indian Foreign Policy." In *The Oxford Handbook of Foreign Policy.* Oxford: Oxford University Press. Available at: https://cpr.unu.edu/a-new-set-of-views-on-indian-foreign-policy.html.

NASSCOM (2015). *IT-BPM Sector in India, Strategic Review 2015.* New Delhi.

OECD (2015). "National Accounts." *OECD.* Available at: http://www.oecd.org/std/na/national-accounts-at-a-glance-22200444.htm.

Safi, M. (2017). "India Launches Record-breaking 104 Satellites from Single Rocket." *The Guardian.* Available at: https://www.theguardian.com/science/2017/feb/15/india-launches-record-breaking-104-satellites-from-single-rocket.

Singh, S. P. (2015) "18 Interesting Facts about India Railways." *Business Standard,* February 16. Available at: http://www.business-standard.com/article/beyond-business/18-interesting-facts-about-india-railways-business-standard-news-115021600404_1.html.

Sircar, S. and Nag, A. (2017). "Record Reserves Turn Costly Cash Pile for India Central Bank." *Bloomberg Markets,* August. Available at: https://www.bloomberg.com/news/articles/2017-08-22/record-reserves-become-costly-cash-pile-for-india-s-central-bank.

Thornhill, T. and Zolfagharifard, E. (2014). "India's Spacecraft Orbits Mars Successfully—and it Cost Less to Send It There Than Hollywood Spent on Making Gravity." Available at: http://www.dailymail.co.uk/sciencetech/article-2767471/India-triumphs-maiden-Mars-mission.html.

Trautmann, T. R. (2015). *India, Brief History of a Civilization*, 2nd edn. Oxford: Oxford University Press.

UN (2017). *Population, United Nations*. Available at: http://www.un.org/en/sections/issues-depth/population/index.html.

WB (2017). *GDP Ranking, PPP Based*. Available at: https://data.worldbank.org/data-catalog/GDP-PPP-based-table.

11

Africa and the Curse of Natural Resources

The world's second largest continent is flush with natural resources, a population over one billion, a rich and vibrant cultural history, and all the elements of a robust economy that still struggles with the basics. Its reliance on natural resources and the lack of management of those resources in a transparent and acceptable manner has led to discontent and conflict. Africa has an opportunity to reboot its economies by embracing value-added positions in the natural resources value chain by providing finished products instead of just the raw material. It could also offer itself as a low-cost manufacturing location to the rest of the world. Signs of more transparent governance and management of resources are being seen in Africa which will eventually lead to a path of growth. Africa's geographical location, in the middle of three major markets; Asia, America, and Europe, gives it an attractive competitive advantage. Africa is poised to drive its emerging economy soundly on to the world stage.

As the second largest continent, with 30 million square kilometers, Africa contains 54 countries with a combined gross domestic product (GDP) of $2.4 trillion and a population of 1.5 billion people. It is rich in natural resources producing 80 percent of the world's platinum, 55 percent of chromite, 49 percent of palladium, 45 percent of vanadium, and 55 percent of gold and diamonds. 57 percent of export earnings in Africa come from hydrocarbons. Africa has proven oil resources of almost 130 billion barrels and gas resources of nearly 14 trillion cubic meters (United Nations Economic Commission for Africa 2016; Murithi 2014). Globalization, in its technology-driven flood, has not left this continent untouched. At first blush then, Africa appears to have all its "ducks." The challenge becomes getting them in a row and seizing the opportunity to become a significant player in the world economy. The delicate balance of legacy, bounty, and opportunity can be a curse or a coronation to a role as a leading global economy.

Legacy

Africa's legacy has been a story of tribal cultures, the ravages of colonization, and integration of western ethos including styles of governance. Mineral resources are certainly an advantage but there has been and still remains issues of leadership that have waylaid the potential. For the most part African leadership has not utilized mineral resources to their full potential and has a lack of will to manage them adequately. Some countries are 100 percent dependent on one mineral resource and must suffer the consequent ramifications of price fluctuations in that resource. If world market prices become volatile, countries suffer the loss of a significant percentage of their earnings and potential purchasing power. For example, Nigeria is a mono-product economy. It is largely oil dependent (Dode 2012). Oil is a double-edged sword that provides opportunities at high market prices and the challenges of scarcity when prices fall.

The feast or famine syndrome in African nations is primarily dependent on their leadership. Natural resources exploited responsibly by leaders, on behalf of the society at large, can create huge amounts of wealth for the society. The fundamental issue is leadership that has the responsibility of translating the intrinsic natural wealth, to shared wealth for the welfare of the society. This is not meant to be a broad condemnation. There is reason for some optimism. Economic growth across the continent in the past three decades, driven largely by the ability to convert natural resources into national connectivity, has produced thinking and positive action around ideas of doing more as a continent. Encouraging initiatives are being pursued that create diversification in economies to supplement the one or two commodities model. Diversification of products, or positioning on the value chain, or targeted sector investment are indicative of the emergence of strengthening leadership.

Governance

Weak leadership has led to armed conflicts in some regions. The issue of blood diamonds in Sierra Leone has led to citizens beginning to ask more questions of governments about utilization of resources (Armstrong 2012). There is evidence of several governments becoming more accountable to their populations. The example of Sierra Leone shows how leadership can emerge from instability, like armed conflicts, and begin focusing on development and proper exploitation of resources. Another reason why conflicts flare up is that members of communities feel disenfranchised from participating in economic value. As an example of the results of the discontent was Botswana's Government changing its process of distributing proceeds from the use of resources more fairly. In the precious gem industry, they use proceeds from sapphires to building a national infrastructure and are developing a social infrastructure that is investing in people through education and health. This has led to a more equitable distribution of the proceeds from minerals and reduced the risk of the disenfranchisement conflict.

Another important area to look at is the environmental consequences of exploiting the natural resources, health issues, and health of the society related to exploitation of natural resources. It is most important to build systems that enable and ensure that natural wealth is appropriately priced for customers that tend to be larger international companies. Smaller countries, like many African nations, must develop or acquire the level of talent to negotiate fair and reasonable contracts. An example is in the commodity space price discount. Some commodities are priced less than market exchanges but in other industries commodity prices are absolute and have more value. The Government's role is to establish policies that create some self-determination in establishing the true value of the commodities, and its aim is to establish an environment that facilitates the conversion of natural wealth into actual value.

Avoiding the Curse

The avoidance of the so-called "curse of natural resources," has been accomplished in some economies such as Canada, Chile, Norway, and Botswana (Durns 2014). For Africa, Botswana is the poster child of economic growth and success. Evidence indicates that other countries are beginning to emulate their example. Again technology becomes a primary player in the dissemination of the Botswana story. Africa is experiencing an increasing flow of information that is inspiring other countries. In Nigeria the new Government is focusing on the eradication of corruption with a push to facilitate increased transparency in the economy. Access to information has resulted in citizens requiring more from their Government. They are asking where the oil resources are going, to what projects, and what infrastructure. The Government is making an effort to be transparent with the hope of directing benefit toward citizens.

One of the greatest contributions of African countries in global trade is the provision of natural resources. If natural wealth can be exploited through responsible, transparent leadership this can provide a massive growth phenomenon to African countries. Africa also has opportunities in terms of its population. With 1.1 billion people it has a large, fresh labor force that is young and growing daily (United Nations Economic Commission for Africa 2016). Economic and political stability are coming to Africa. In terms of population Africa is a huge market. It is not just a large workforce but a big consumer market. Many companies in mature markets are searching for growth opportunities and Africa represents consumer potential in various sectors such as telecommunications and other sectors, such as health, that have not been yet explored in any depth. With the potential for one of the largest middle-class segments globally there is phenomenal opportunity. Not only does the middle class provides a vast market opportunity for international trade but there is opportunity as well at the bottom of the pyramid. As borders continue to open within existing trade zones, West, Southern, and Easter Africa, coupled with improved communication, there will be immense potential in the continent as well as globally. Africa's potential in global trade is further enhanced by the fact that it was part of the Commonwealth network of countries. It has many English-speaking professionals that easily provide language and cultural bridges between western corporations, western markets, and African companies and markets. In addition, there is Africa's geographical location, located as it is right in the middle three major markets, India, America, and Europe. Exploiting Africa's location for the creation of regional and global supply chain may unveil another dramatic advantage. It could become the global hub for logistics.

Many big cities in African countries are experiencing rapid urbanization. With that, comes an enormous demand for water and solid waste management. This creates broad market openings for the whole industry of environment management, which is an opportunity for western countries with numerous corporations specializing in the sector.

International Support

At the end of the Obama administration (in the United States) the Africa Growth Opportunity Act was enacted. Under this initiative important African country members and those seeking market access to the US markets can locate some operations in Africa and duty free markets in the United States (Office of the United States Trade Representative 2016). Recently, the Southern African Development Community (SADC), comprising 14 member nation-states within the Southern Africa economic zone, negotiated an economic partnership agreement with the European Union (EU) enabling potential access, without restrictions, to quota and duty free markets, for member countries into the EU (European Commission 2016).

Africa presents manufacturing capacity for companies searching for locations in low-cost manufacturing environments. From the policy perspective there is evidence of a growing trend to create an environment more conducive to business development. African governments are recognizing the fact that business is attracted to predictable and stable environments for companies to produce and compete. There is a general movement toward competitiveness by many African governments based on the "ease of doing business" rankings done by the World Bank and the global competitiveness rankings by the World Economic Forum (The Global Competitiveness Report 2016–2017, 2016).

Africa is now poised to export many value-added products and transactions have already begun. For example, Botswana has several joint ventures with international companies around the transfer of technology and value addition is taking place in the natural mineral industries. One way to increase the participation of Africa in the context of global trade would be to add more value to local products. Today Africa provides an opportunity for developing innovative solutions because there are so many unresolved problems faced by society whether in the field of nutrition, or health, or pharmaceuticals. Africa can become a primary market for prototyping innovations. Many global pharmaceutical companies have undertaken vaccine research programs and the development of nutritious products. If this message of innovation travels around the world there may be many more of these initiatives. It even opens up the possibility of African production exported around the world.

Local Value Addition

For far too long as countries and a continent, Africa has relied on the extractive end of the value chain. With that role they have exported a lot of value in terms of jobs and economic activity which are part and parcel of a value-added economy. The emerging revelation that adding worth may be more valuable than resource extraction is gaining advocates. Botswana partnered with the diamond industry's De Beers to relocate civil and education functions from London to Botswana (Davies 2013). They are also creating a diamond cutting and polishing industry with existing companies in Botswana. The aspiration is to move further up in the value chain for jewelry manufacturing and to provide more finished products. A separate sales channel distinct from other activities of the company would be created to aggregate and sell through an independent company in Botswana. This effectively empowers the country by increasing experience and exposure to diamond markets internationally. Value-adding locations within Africa creates huge opportunities for local employment. For example, Nigeria ships its fresh fruits to Europe. 35 percent of all cut flower imports into the EU come from Kenya (Kenya Flower Council 2016). Produce exports creates hundreds of thousands of jobs locally for the African people. It creates the opportunity for middle-class expansion which is the foundation for further development. Realistically, African governments have shown their leadership in creating environments, negotiating trade deals, and empowering citizens to benefit in the long term. These examples are evidence of the transformation in the political space.

Changing Scenario

Several African countries have learned from past mistakes, and can now boast of stable governments and a smoother transition from one ruling cabinet to the next through the democratic election process. This has improved the reputation and credibility of African countries and African corporations tremendously. A positive trend sees enlightened leaders from African countries and evidence that Africa is moving to take a major role in shaping not just the trends in international trade but also policies. The change in leadership thinking is enabling fair compensation, conversion of natural wealth to value, and finished products and services. There are examples of this change all over Africa. For the first time in their history Nigeria has had an opposition party leader voted into office (Lee 2015). More African countries are joining the ranks of countries like Ghana, Mauritius, Namibia, and Botswana, where there are very smooth transitions of power and free and fair elections. This precipitates a rise in confidence on the part of international investors that recognize the leveling of the playing field.

Africa looks to global players as enablers for economic growth and prosperity. These players are multinationals who are encouraged to take a closer look at Africa, its resources, products, people, and potential. They are encouraged to examine its legacy and evolution from one-source economies to value-added markets. Presenting opportunities for public-private partnerships, many African countries can nurture efficient capital markets and the banking systems have matured in many countries. The basic building blocks of creating innovative organizations, namely constitutional provisions and regulatory structures, are now in place. An amount of investment has gone into public-private partnerships to provide safe drinking water to the people living in different parts of Africa. Public-private partnerships are evident in the energy sector, and in the development of ports and railway infrastructure. As long as governments and the private sector can trust each other and are willing to share their risk, and as long as there are efficient mechanisms to support any form of business activity, there is real potential for the rest of the world to invest in Africa.

Infrastructure is improving. In energy there is still a deficit in the continent's electrical grid. Governments across the continent are becoming more open to renewable energy such as solar and wind energy. Another key sector is agriculture. A huge percentage of urban land in Africa remains untapped yet it does not produce enough food to feed the continent. There must be commercialization of large scale agriculture production and processing. Though there has been significant investment by governments across Africa in technology infrastructure, opportunities still abound. Tourism is another sector that is significantly unexploited and could attract investment. Africa has the opportunity to move to the world stage as a significant part of the global economy.

References

Armstrong, P. (2012). *Sierra Leone "Blood Diamonds" Not Forever*, BBC. Available at: http://www.cnn.com/2012/04/26/world/africa/blood-diamonds/index.html (Accessed: 22 November 2017).

Davies, R. (2013). "A Diamond in the Rough: De Beers could be Anglo-American's Gem even with Mining's High Costs." *This is Money.* Available at: http://www.thisismoney.co.uk/money/markets/article-2491218/CITY-FOCUS-De-Beers-Anglo-Americans-gem-rough-times.html.

Dode, R. (2012). "Nigeria, Mono-Product Economy & The Global Economic Recession: Problems & Prospects." *Global Journal of Human Social* 12(11): 3. Available at: https://globaljournals.org/GJHSS_Volume12/6-Nigeria-Mono-Product-Economy.pdf.

Durns, S. (2014). "Four Countries that Beat the Resource Curse." *Global Risk Insights.* Available at: http://globalriskinsights.com/2014/04/four-countries-that-beat-the-resource-curse/.

European Commission (2017). "Putting Partnership into Practice, Economic Partnership Agreements (PEAs) between the EU and African, Caribbean and Pacific (ACP) Countries." European Commission Publications Office.

Kenya Flower Council (2016). "Kenya's Flower Exports to Remain Steady in 2017." Available at: http://www.xinhuanet.com/english/2017-05/04/c_136254745.htm.

Lee, K. (2015). "Nigerian Opposition Leader Buhari Wins the Presidency: Why this is a Big Deal." *Vox*, March. Available at: https://www.vox.com/2015/3/31/8320577/nigeria-election-opposition-win.

Murithi, T. (2014). *Handbook of Africa's International Relations*. London: Routledge.

Office of the United States Trade Representative (2016). *African Growth and Opportunity Act (AGOA)*. Available at: https://ustr.gov/sites/default/files/2016-AGOA-Implementation-Report.pdf.

The Global Competitiveness Report 2016–2017 (2016). Available at: http://www3.weforum.org/docs/GCR2016-2017/05FullReport/TheGlobalCompetitivenessReport2016-2017_FINAL.pdf.

United Nations Economic Commission for Africa (2016). *The Demographic Profile of African Countries, United Nations Economic Commission for Africa, March 2016*. Addis Ababa: United Nations Economic Commission for Africa.

12

Australia—The Hidden Jewel

With the twenty-first century being touted as the Asian century, is there an opportunity for Australia to take a significant place in the global economy? With its stable economy, good governance, education system, and above all the natural resource abundance, will it become more entrepreneurial in future and accelerate the rate of growth or will it get infected with Dutch disease (i.e. the negative impact on an economy based on anything that gives rise to a sharp inflow of foreign currency, such as the discovery of significant oil reserves. The currency inflows lead to currency appreciation, making the country's other products less price competitive on the export market (Grene 2008))? It has been successful in managing trade ties with fast-developing economies like China and India as well as developed countries like the United States. It has participated in the growth of China by providing iron ore and coal. As a low-risk country, it has enabled inflow of significant foreign capital investments. A lot will depend on its capability and willingness to invest the capital available in entrepreneurial ventures, its ability to capture the full value chain of natural resources, and to export the finished products instead of raw materials, while building a robust manufacturing sector.

The Current Situation

Today the world's economy is increasingly Asia-driven and, as this book has shown in its examples of emerging markets, three of them are Asian. While China and India have notable socioeconomic trajectories, Africa and Australia both have significant potential. In this chapter we examine the hidden jewel of the global economy, Australia. Its location and close integration with Asia is instrumental for Australia's future along with its stable economy, strong education, export, and capital. Australia is a continent on its own, and the sixth largest country in the world. It is an island whose isolation from the rest of the world boasts over 750 different reptile species, more than any other country. It has a population of 23.2 million, a GDP of $1.18 trillion, a growth rate of 2.5 percent (CIA 2016). Australia's economy is the twelfth largest globally and it straddles emerging and developed markets. As the biggest iron ore exporter and a major supplier of coal, wool, gold, and liquefied natural gas, its fortunes are wedded to its main export partner, China (Bloomberg 2016). This South Pacific nation is about more than raw materials, it has a thriving tourism industry with education being a major economic driver. Australia's low regulatory environment, transparency, and efficiency are all conducive to entrepreneurial development (Anon 2016a).

Its stable political climate supports transparent, well-established political process, a strong legal system, effective competent governments, and an independent bureaucracy adds to its allure. In 1980 the global economic center of gravity was mid-Atlantic. Unsurprisingly that reflected the fact that North America and Western Europe held the greatest portion of the world economic activity. By 2008 that center of gravity drifted to a location east of Helsinki and Bucharest. This change occurred because of the continued rise of China and Asia. It is the rise of the East that has pulled the global economy center of gravity almost three-quarters eastwards around the world. Extrapolating growth in those nearly 700 locations across the earth, the economic center of gravity by 2050 is projected to be between India and China (Quah 2011). What this means for Australia is an indicator of its potential to be a major player in Asia and with other developed economies.

The Global Connection

By just about all measures, the twenty-first century is the Asian century. APEC members accounted for 71.1 percent of Australia's total trade, ASEAN members accounted for 13.8 percent, members of the European Union (EU) accounted for 14.6 percent, G20 members accounted for 69.6 percent, and OECD countries accounted for 44.7 percent. China was Australia's largest export destination (valued at $93.0 billion) and import source (valued at $62.1 billion). Australia is well-placed geographically, well-placed in raw materials, well positioned socioeconomically, in areas of free trade agreements and education services, and it has a history of engagement with Asia and other countries globally. The growth in China driven by its infrastructure building has spiked Australian iron and energy exports. Iron ore and coal are Australia's two largest resources, exported primarily to China, and have propelled the Chinese growth in infrastructure (Anon. 2016b).

Key Drivers

As a result of Australia's raw materials, geography, and socioeconomic positioning, it has taken advantage of the markets as a primary producer and exporter. Unfortunately, it has also developed a culture around that situation and lacks in the development of value-added initiatives. With only 23 million people and the significant investment required to develop a manufacturing sector, it has been difficult to build that with a limited number of individuals. Agricultural and mining have been the key drivers of the economy and since the going has been good in those sectors, there is little motivation for Australia to move into value-added processing.

Australia's output goes beyond volume. It is noted for its outstanding quality whether in agricultural practices, food safety laws, or health, safety, and security in the mining industries. This is the good news. The downside is that any qualitative parameter of excellence does not build preference if you are purely a commodity player. In the commodities market competition is global and if prices in Brazil or Russia, irrespective of quality, are cheaper, then the business goes elsewhere. The opportunity may not be building any capital-intensive industries reliant on a small population base but might be to take advantage of existing strengths, such as agriculture, to create value-adding processing that will expand and stabilize their economic base. People associate the brand Australia with excellent reliability and quality, but Australia has very few national brands.

Capital Inflow

There is an ongoing political and emotive debate about the correct level of foreign investment, for example, Chinese investment in the cattle and agriculture industries, in the infrastructure industry, and the mining sector. This investment has, for the most part, been welcome, however for various reasons, both political and protectionist, the capital inflow has fueled debates. The reality is that capital inflow is needed to stimulate the growth of industry. The balance of investment between Australia and Asia has grown tremendously. In the last ten years the Asian inflow has increased almost 50 percent and the Australian outflow has increased by nearly 200 percent (Trading Economics 2016). Australia is a net importer of capital. Australians seem to be a little weary of putting capital overseas. However, they lack the mindset and skills to compete with Asians who are far more entrepreneurial and trust their money in Australia because of its stability, laws, and level playing field. They are also far more open minded when it comes to taking opportunity risks.

Australia has more than $2 trillion in their super funds, or pension funds which are managed professionally, that are poised for potential investments in infrastructure development in India, Indonesia, and perhaps other Southeast Asian countries (Mason 2015). However, with Australia's ageing population there is pressure to see money as a commodity and find investment options to look for yield rather than capital appreciation and safety (Mason 2015). The low risk investment appetite in Australia could be a positive for Asian countries who are looking for low risk environments for investment.

Natural Resources and Business

The advantage of being a resource-rich country with a low risk affinity has had positive effects on almost every level of society but it has had some negative consequences too. Looking ahead a few years, the era of finite natural resources must begin to sunset at some point and, with technological advances in alternative energies, the demand for natural energy resources will diminish significantly. Stability and conservatism also leads to an excess of risk aversion and certain blindness or myopia to what is happening in the wider environment. This has resulted in some parochialism and monopolistic tendencies that have a deleterious effect on the continuing development and systemic retooling needed to stay relevant in the globalized world.

Like Africa, Australia is also a resource-rich country with it primary economic driver being the export of those resources (CIA 2016). There is a need to focus on other sector development to broaden the sole source reliance. There is some evidence that the country is making significant efforts to shore up or develop new pillars in their economy. The service sector is strengthening as is food and agriculture exports. The manufacturing sector, however, requires some rethinking. The highly monopolistic environment in Australia creates problems of internal thinking which tends to exclude or slow down innovation, limits access to venture growth capital, leads financial institutions to become risk averse and lend mostly into established more monopolistic assets. As an example, an indicator of a growing healthy economy is the evolution of its top performing businesses. In the past 75 years of the top ten performing companies in the United States, only two remain on the list with the other eight being replaced. In India it is two out of ten. In Australia, of the ten companies listed at the outset, eight remain on the list. Admittedly this stable conservatism is comforting to the Australian psyche but it may eventually have a negative effect. Monopolistic thinking looks inward and move slowly or not at all, it believes it is not vulnerable, cannot be penetrated, and sees its future as secured. This is not a condemnation but a confirmation that there is recognition in the system that changes need to happen and there are strategies being deployed to facilitate evolutionary change.

Education and Entrepreneurship

One of the most valuable natural resources in Australia is human intellect, much of which is imported from Asia. The Australian education system is excellent but there is a need for entrepreneurial energy. There are, however, signs that such energy is being ignited. ROBE, an oil seed, crushing, and refining company is barely four years old and boasts a larger oil refining capability and capacity than the global giant Cargill. This is a result of the significant intervention by the Government enabling connectivity to Asia and disseminating a positive image of doing business in Australia. Adding to the pre-emptive nature of the entrepreneurial argument from a global perspective is the growth of the middle class in places like China, India, and worldwide. Combined with population expansion, the demand for consumer goods will go up as will income growth. This adds credence to the argument for entrepreneurial energy leading to economic diversification.

Getting Old and Rich

Australian demographics show that the population is getting older and wealthier. This may represent some risk without the expansion of the demographic base. The disproportionate number of seniors will put strain on younger taxpayers and government. Extended longevity will stretch the health services and pension system.

Australians have also become richer with the average net worth rising almost 40 percent in the last ten years. They have been accumulating wealth rapidly with a savings rate of 11 percent of disposable income (ATKearney 2014). As mentioned earlier, super funds or pension funds sit at over $2 trillion (Mason 2015). The question becomes the fiduciary responsibility during the time of capital reserves. The risk averse approach provides strong balance but is also unproductive in terms of fueling the economic evolution. The significant expansion of capital through a capital appreciation rather than of income does not take full advantage of the inherent power of capital. Also, Australia's economy has been among the most stable in the world. It was one of the few countries that was not impacted by the 2008 global financial crisis. Real estate has appreciated between three and four times in the last 20 years and there has been no boom and bust in housing. This is fueled by immigration from Asia and capital appreciation. At the same time, though costs have risen, hourly wages have also increased enabling the buying power of consumers to remain relatively constant.

The Australian psyche likes a stable environment. This trait can be seen as a detriment to their global positioning, or as a dramatic advantage. This jewel of the Pacific has the potential of emerging as a major economic power in Asia and on the world stage based almost entirely on the choices they make in the future.

References

Anon. (2016a). *Composition of Trade*. Available at: http://dfat.gov.au/about-us/publica tions/Documents/cot-cy-2016.pdf.

Anon. (2016b). "Index of Economic Freedom." *Heritage Foundation*. Available at: http:// www.heritage.org/index/country/australia.

ATKearney (2014). "Banking on Our Future: Framing a Vision for the Australian Banking Industry." *ATKearney*. Available at: https://www.atkearney.com/financial-institutions/featured-article/-/asset_publisher/j8IucAqMqEhB/content/banking-on-our-future-framing-a-vision-for-the-australian-banking-industry/10192.

Bloomberg (2016). "AUD Surge May Signal Good Times for the Global Economy." *Bloomberg*. Available at: https://au.finance.yahoo.com/news/aud-surge-may-signal-good-times-for-the-global-economy-001626169.html.

CIA (2016). "The CIA World Factbook." Available at: https://www.cia.gov/library/publications/the-world-factbook/geos/.

Grene, S. (2008). "Investors Sign Up to a Better World." *Financial Times*. Available at: https://www.ft.com/content/1f55834a-186c-11dd-8c92-0000779fd2ac.

Mason, R. (2015). *The Dynamics of a $9.5 Trillion Australian Super System*. Available at: https://www2.deloitte.com/au/en/pages/media-releases/articles/dynamics-of-9-5-tril lion-australian-super-system-171115.html.

Quah, D. (2011). "The Global Economy's Shifting Centre of Gravity." *Global Policy* 2(1): 3–9.

Trading Economics (2016). "Australia Capital Flows." *Trading Economics*. Available at: https://tradingeconomics.com/australia/capital-flows.

Part III
The Tumultuous World

13

Geopolitical Upheavals: Brexit and Trump

In recent years, investments had been going down, living standards had deteriorated, and inequality had risen. The underlying disaffection was picked up by Brexit and the Trump campaigns. Although these problems were not the inevitable results of globalization, but rather of domestic policy choices influenced by flawed economic theories, these populist standard bearers exploited it by blaming those challenges on external forces, including globalization. The Brexit vote and the election of Trump can be considered as the voice of the economically "left behind," a protest by working-class voters at the impact of globalization on their jobs and living standards.

Those voters chose Trump or Brexit as the solution to their problems. In the United States, median household incomes are basically the same today as they were a quarter of a century ago, even though gross domestic product (GDP) has grown by almost 80 percent over this period. In the United Kingdom there has been a similar divergence between median income and GDP growth over this long period; it is only since the financial crisis that the stagnation of wages has been really noticeable. The median household disposable income in 2014–15 was back to its level of 2007–08. In no region of the United Kingdom, outside of London and the Southeast, is output back to its pre-crisis levels. At the same time the incomes of the richest 1 percent in both countries have continued to surge ahead. In the first three years of the US recovery after 2008, an extraordinary 91 percent of the gains in income went to the richest one-hundredth of the population (Jacobs and Mazzucato 2016).

Brexit

Brexit is a commonly used term for the United Kingdom's planned withdrawal from the European Union (EU). Following the 2016 referendum vote to leave, the UK Government started the withdrawal process on 29 March 2017, putting it on course to leave by April 2019 (Marks and Paravicini 2017). Brexit may tighten the financial conditions and lower consumer investor confidence in Europe and the United Kingdom and create uncertainties in emerging market economies. It might affect the fragile bubble of growth in developed economies like Japan and the United States, but the effect seems minimal while in China there seems to be no effect at all. However, if the growth in advanced economies deteriorates, China might well be affected.

Implications

For currency trade, the implications may be far reaching. Brexit represents a country that no longer wants to be part of a trading block. The consequences on trade, not only for the United Kingdom and the EU but more broadly, could be significant. The issue is linkages in the global economy and the extent to which countries desire participation in larger trade blocks or groups.

Other than trade, the impact on services and the uncertainty for the City of London are still in the speculation phase. Large American and Asian global financial companies use London as their European headquarters, facilitating easier access and provision of services to Europe. Their ability to pass services from London to Europe is now uncertain along with the potential for moving large parts of the workforce to another city in Europe. This will affect London and the United Kingdom's financial industry as well as its position as a financial center.

The impact on currency, as the pound sterling becomes weaker or stronger against the dollar and the Euro, is another uncertainty. It is possible that the United Kingdom and the EU have opened a Pandora's Box for investors with lower commodity prices, bond yields, and hesitation around investments from emerging markets. It has created both short- and long-term uncertainty. Though there was a short-term effect on currency with the pound falling against the dollar and the Euro, the International Monetary Fund (IMF) expects the dollar and pound to find equilibrium going forward (Weeks 2016).

There is another important long-term potential implication of Brexit on the investment markets. To what extent will investors treat the United Kingdom differently once it is outside the EU? The question in the long term will be, do investors continue to value the pound sterling as an asset and continue to fund both trade and fiscal spending by buying from the UK Government. In the longer term, will investors want to own sterling-based assets. For example, the London property market is popular globally and though investors enjoy traveling from London and owning property in a cosmopolitan setting, if they see the pound sterling as a currency with potential to depreciate they must ask themselves if they really want to own these assets.

The Financial Center

It took decades of discussions to build the EU, to give it a structure that unraveled the entanglement of so many countries, policies, and government bodies. The financial industry in which the United Kingdom had a major role remains the place where all of the financial transactions are completed. This change could trigger a move from global financial companies who have previously headquartered in the United Kingdom. Europe benefits greatly from being well-integrated and having London as its financial center. London has a deep connection to growing capital markets and serves as a gateway for global financial markets. They do it in a way that Paris and Frankfurt have really never been able to do. The potential of that relationship between the United Kingdom and the EU is growing more complex and the possibility of any reduction in access would obviously reduce the attractiveness of the United Kingdom to the overall European capital market.

Impact on the Economy

There will be an impact on GDP and the European economy if there is a reduction in trade and increase in the cost of trade between the United Kingdom and the rest of Europe. It will be damaging to both sides. The greatest burden will be on the large economies like Germany that may have to add €2.5 billion to the current €30 billion already in the EU budget (Marks and Paravicini 2017). That is bound to impact the cost of trade and services as well as GDP and the EU budget. The untethered movement of the workforce will have repercussions on labor costs and cost of production likely to rise with the United Kingdom finding themselves producing less competitive products.

Another possible impact on the European economy is the potential diminished perception of the European capital market to the extent that corporations and global businesses that want to raise money view Europe in the same way without London. This is an important question for the United Kingdom and the EU, which have benefited in the recent years from a maturation of the capital market which has historically relied on bank lending and other forms of traditional financing and more capital market-oriented solutions for finance. Without London as its center, the European economy will suffer for some time.

Trading Partners

During the Brexit campaign, one of the benefits argued by the Leave campaigners was the ability the United Kingdom would have to strike bilateral agreements with countries with much more freedom and flexibility than from inside the Union. However, the reality is that a country tends to trade most with countries that are closest to it. The United States has Canada as its foremost trade partner, for example (WTO 2017). That is also the case with the United Kingdom and the EU and although they will have the freedom to strike bilateral trade agreements with countries such as Australia or Canada or other respective Commonwealth countries the reality is that the trade linkages, when they are that far-flung, tend to be lower.

We will continue to see uncertainty in the short and medium term, which will affect global growth. In the short term, we see that emerging markets will benefit. In the short and medium term, there will be an expectation, because of a weaker dollar and lower rates in emerging markets, of a disruptive effect on trade as Brexit has created a positive momentum for emerging markets and emerging markets' assets.

Financial Markets

From a financial market perspective in the short term, there will be little impact. For the longer term, it will depend on what kind of agreement is struck between the EU and the United Kingdom. Whether we end up with a constructive compromise or a divorce, both will have significant ramifications for future trade. It is hardly surprising that an economic system which distributes its rewards so badly should lose its popular legitimacy. It is a phenomenon which may well be repeated in European elections over the next few years. The political beneficiaries may be unable to address their voters' concerns. Like the movement mobilized by Donald Trump in the United States, the Five Star Alliance in Italy, Podemos in Spain, the Front National in France, the Corbyn phenomenon in the United Kingdom, and the Law and Justice Party in Poland, Brexit represented the collective efforts of those "left behind" in Britain to protect themselves from the predatory nature of market fundamentalism of deployment of orthodox economics (Weeks 2016).

There is no roadmap to follow or analogy to invoke as a guide or pattern for how the Brexit vote will reverberate in the months and years to come. However, a few immediate consequences seem highly likely. The flight to safety away from the epicenter of this British-EU divorce will push capital away from the region and toward key safe-haven markets including the United States, especially Treasuries, and to Japan. This will further lower market interest rates and raise relative currency values (Marks and Paravicini 2017).

Trump Victory

Months after the United Kingdom unexpectedly voted to leave the EU, the world got another shock at the ballot box when Donald Trump defied the polls and conventional wisdom and was elected President of the United States. Like Brexit, Trump's election seemed to be a rebuke to globalization and the conventions of the post-war order. The most substantial concern for the global business environment at this point of time is uncertainty, regarding both policies and key personnel.

Trump has called for 45 percent customs duties on a swath of products from China, 35 percent duties on products from Mexico, and 15–35 percent duties on products from other countries deemed "currency manipulators" (Global Network Perspectives (GNP) 2016). If such protectionist tariffs were imposed, they would inflict real damage on the US retail sector—especially stores such as Wal-Mart that import the majority of their consumer products from China. Ultimately, the US middle- and working-class consumers would have to pay more for everyday goods as well as having fewer choices.

Impact on Global Business

Trump's election has ushered in an era of heightened uncertainty and anxiety in global business. It is not clear how far Trump will go to carry out his campaign pledges. Imposing high tariffs against goods originating from Mexico, China, and (potentially) the EU, Japan, and Korea could have devastating effects on production networks and business ecosystems. A worst case scenario would include a trade war between the United States and China, the world's two largest economies, whereby the Chinese impose retaliatory tariffs on US goods and services. Even if no trade war occurs, protectionist tariffs will severely disrupt global value chains of not only US and Chinese firms, but also thousands of foreign subsidiaries that have embedded themselves in cross-border production networks. If Trump policies disrupt these value chains, it is likely that many US firms and US-based foreign subsidiaries will relocate their activities elsewhere, creating the exact opposite outcome than that which was intended. Global cities like Singapore, which function as trade and financial centers, could likely experience, first, a slow-down from the effects of the Trump-induced trade fallout, followed by heightened activity, as US firms and other multinationals move their operations out of the United States to Asia (Global Network Perspectives 2016).

In terms of the global business environment, there will be much stronger rhetoric coming from the United States to an extent; it is true that the expansion of economies in East and Southeast Asia came at the heavy expense of a subset of the populace in the United States. It is also true that US manufacturing is recovering, becoming more productive, and leaving less reason for US firms to outsource or seek manufacturing partnerships outside their domestic market. As much as ever, East and South-east Asian economies need the cooperative United States, more than the United States needs the cooperation of these economies. Increasingly, policy makers as a whole understand these positions, which means terms of trade, trade negotiations, trade treaties, and perhaps even the action of individual firms, will leverage this strength in their bargaining position more so than they have in the past, extracting terms that are more favorable to US firms.

Trump's election will impact South Africa via the global financial and trade channels rather than directly. Short-term trade negotiations are likely to be difficult, but the long-term trade agreements are unlikely to be affected. Aid programs, including USAID, anti-HIV/AIDS programs, etc., may be scaled back, which will have social implications. The Johannesburg Stock Exchange will be impacted by the companies with international listings rather than by the locally domiciled listings, and the bond market will be affected by the US interest rate and deficit spending (Global Network Perspectives (GNP) 2016).

Trump plans to boost the US economy through an expanded infrastructure program but the budgetary reallocation to do so is problematic because if government spending increases then this will lead to inflationary pressure necessitating interest rate increases.

Trump's victory is seen with trepidation from Spain. His anti-globalization rhetoric promises that trade agreements will be scrapped, and protectionism will prevail over freer trade. Spain exited its recession thanks to export growth, and a trade slowdown hurts its prospects and those of the world. On the upside, Spanish companies could win contracts in Trump's infrastructure program, and the stronger dollar may boost Eurozone exports and induce more Americans to vacation in Spain (Global Network Perspectives 2016).

Businessman Wins in a Democratic Process

American politics have long been a source of consternation and entertainment, and the recent election cycle has proved true to form. From the world's perspective, this has been theater at its best. The election of Donald Trump to arguably the most powerful position in the world was both surprising and curious. A lot has been said during the election process about the Trump style of working, his political and business acumen. The reality facing the world is that he is the democratically elected President of the United States of America, the most powerful nation in the world. Trump projected himself as a successful businessman during the election process. He fought internal party strife and his political opponents; fueled by millions of dollars of free media, revolutionizing the American political paradigm. Trump translated his opposition into fuel for his campaign. He rallied thousands, if not millions at his rallies across the country. His power of personality translated into massive rallies and eventually his electoral win; a factor pollsters and pundits never took into account. His cult of personality combined with his "never quit" attitude resulted in one of the greatest political upsets in modern American history.

The China Factor

Trump has been pretty unequivocal about China throughout his campaign. The United States is the biggest single market for Chinese exports accounting for about 20 percent of the total (Hsu 2017). There would be a risk that aggressive US trade policy could result in a marked slowdown in China's growth and a loss of manufacturing jobs. Faced with that possibility, Beijing would have two choices. It might take an emollient line, promising to increase direct investment into the United States as a way of supporting Trump's attempt to rebuild the American economy. More likely though, China would adopt an aggressive nationalistic stance. Beijing is not without its own economic weapons since it has amassed a vast stock of US Treasury bonds in recent years, the proceeds of its trade surplus with America. Beijing could meet Trump's threat with one of its own: to dump US assets. A tit-for-tat trade war, in which China puts tariffs on US exports, could not be ruled out either (Xin and Yu 2017).

Change from the Past

President Obama saw trade agreements with Asia as a way of keeping countries such as Japan, Brunei, Singapore, and Malaysia out of Beijing's orbit. All these countries have an export-led model of growth and Obama's plan was to create a US-led free trade zone that included all the major economies of the Pacific apart from China. That plan now lies in tatters (Elliott 2016). The Trump presidency has signaled that countries such as South Korea and Taiwan will be subject to the same protectionist structures as Mexico and China. This would result in slower growth across Asia as exports and investment weaken. Japan, which has been in the doldrums for a quarter of a century and which remains on the brink of deflation, appears to be most at risk, but it is not alone in being anxious about the impact of Trump. In geopolitical terms, a tough US trade stance provides China with the opportunity to increase its influence in the region, bolstering economic ties, and making countries of the Pacific Rim less dependent on the American market (Global Network Perspectives (GNP) 2016).

Impact on Europe

The main short-term risk to Europe, excluding Britain, looks to be political rather than economic. Matteo Renzi's left of center government may struggle to win a referendum on constitutional change in Italy. The elections in Germany, France, and the Netherlands had a strong right wing showing where parties of the right were looking to surf the populist tide that carried Trump to his win. There will be nervousness in the Baltic states of Latvia, Lithuania, and Estonia regarding the possibility that Russia will be emboldened by Trump's apparent isolationism. There are, however, economic and financial implications for Europe. Like Asia, the Eurozone is heavily reliant on exports as a source of growth. These could be affected in two ways: through a more restrictive US trade regime and if a weaker dollar drives up the Euro on the foreign exchanges. The relative calm of financial markets immediately after Trump's victory will come as a great relief to European banks, which look highly vulnerable to a sustained bout of the jitters.

The United Kingdom will not be immune from any slowdown in the global economy that might result from a Trump victory. Britain is the second biggest exporter of services in the world and America takes more of them than any other country. But Trump's protectionist measures are targeted at cheap manufactured goods, rather than the high-end services Britain provides, and Trump's win helps take the pressure off the pound. Sterling has been sold heavily against the dollar since the EU referendum, partly because of uncertainty about what the United Kingdom will look like after Brexit. Trump's victory brings risk and uncertainty into the equation for the United States as well (Elliott 2016).

Trump's America

If President Trump manages to keep America out of an immediate economic crisis, the long-run effects of his presidency will prove most profound. The status of many international institutions is now in question. It is hard to imagine new trade deals being completed, and old ones might be reopened or scrapped. Trump has some leeway to unilaterally impose temporary trade restrictions, but such moves would entitle other countries to respond with punitive restrictions of their own. One suspects that Trump will not be especially interested in international cooperation to limit tax avoidance or restrain the power of global banks. It is possible that a Trump administration would pull support from the IMF and the World Bank, removing some of the shock absorbers in the international system. He has promised to reduce regulation, but it is hard to know how he will manage significant economic trends, like consolidation in American industry. It is easy to see him as a corporatist, willing to give lots of room for maneuver to powerful firms. That could be good for profits, while also encouraging economic nationalism around the world, undermining the long-run growth potential of the American economy, and reducing the bargaining power of workers (*The Economist* 2016).

President Trump controls the world's most powerful military. It is hard to know how he will use it, or the diplomatic machinery of the American Government. Any move toward greater conflict in the Middle East or Asia could have severe economic consequences: from soaring oil prices to market panic to interruptions in global trade.

A rise in American and worldwide protectionism, however, would not be a "trend breaker," but the intensification of an existing trend. Since the beginning of this century, the global trade agenda has been moribund. The WTO Doha Development Round launched in 2001 was thwarted at the Cancún ministerial conference in 2003. In 2005, The Evian Group warned that Doha was a dying duck (Global Network Perspectives 2016). This was stridently denied by most policy makers, who then and for the ensuing years have engaged not in thinking the unthinkable but in wishful thinking. Doha is dead! Whereas Trump is an overt protectionist, the trade policy makers in the administration of his two predecessors, George Bush and Barack Obama, were closet protectionists. The main obstacle to pursuing an open rules-based multilateral trade agenda has arisen due to the inability of the former dominant actors, the United States, Europe, and Japan, to adjust to the emergence of new players, especially China, but also other emerging economies.

The most recent blatant manifestation of this failure has been the "mega-regionals," notably the Transatlantic Trade and Investment Partnership (TTIP) and Trans Pacific Partnership (TPP), both of which flagrantly discriminate against the new actors China, India, Brazil, and South Africa.

Features of the Brexit and Trump Victories

In the end, it is evident from these perspectives that both the Brexit and Trump victories are unprecedented and have the potential to have a major impact on the global economy. It has created an uncertainty and expectations divergent from normal. The similarities, in Brexit and the Trump election, however, aren't exact. The main feature is that the campaigns shared a tendency to blame external forces for domestic economic problems. The rise in inequality and the loss of skilled jobs over the last four decades, which have propelled Brexit and Trump, resulted not from the unstoppable forces of globalization. They are the result of current political, policy, and business choices. These options need to be questioned along with the problematic economic theory which has influenced them.

Globalization and technological change did not need to lead to the hollowing out of skilled jobs and downward pressure on median incomes on the scale that has occurred in the United States or the United Kingdom. It is governments' ability to shape and create markets and to negotiate their terms and conditions that determine the kind of economy that emerges from these global and technological forces. The tragedy of globalization over the last thirty years is that it has occurred at the same time as the dominance of an economic orthodoxy that saw the state retreat from active economic management. Maybe what was needed more active states redistributing its rewards to develop the productive economy and to ensure fairer outcomes.

Austerity since the financial crash has focused on the size of annual deficits, rather than on the composition of public spending and the contribution it can make to long-term growth. This problem is compounded by the orthodox economic view that limits the role of public policy in correcting market failures. Firms are assumed to be ready and willing to invest, with the role of policy limited to removing the barriers that might be inhibiting them from doing so. Yet, investment firms have focused on shareholder value seeing corporations' return of cash to shareholders in record amounts to boost share prices rather than reinvest in future productive capacity. In the decade from 2003 to 2012, the largest 500 companies returned more than $2.4 trillion to shareholders in the form of share buybacks. Today, more than $2 trillion of idle cash is sitting on the books of public companies in the United States, rather than being reinvested, with a further €2 trillion in Europe (Jacobs and Mazzucato 2016). The orthodox economic theory has guided poor economic policy.

Role of Financial Markets

For more than 40 years, the prevailing economic consensus has been that financial markets are efficient, corporations will best innovate and invest when left to themselves, rising inequality is the price to be paid for growth, and the best role for government is to get smaller. The great financial crash and the profound failure of the austerity policies which followed it did not change the orthodox economic consensus. Unregulated financial markets are prone to misallocating resources and creating asset bubbles which inevitably burst. Corporations and financial asset holders seeking to maximize shareholder value tend to under-invest in long-term growth.

Innovation is best galvanized through a partnership of public and private finance. Public investment banks can crowd in private capital when demand is weak. Unequal economies tend to have worse growth performance. Governments need to adopt a much more proactive economic strategy of supporting investment-led growth, using fiscal powers, labor market regulation, public investment, and "mission-oriented" market creation to shape economic development. They should also think much more creatively about how to socialize not only the risks but the rewards of investments they have supported. In areas like drug pricing, patent laws, and the financing of innovation, the state has been far too willing to take the costs while allowing the private sector to reap the benefits. If policy makers are to respond in better ways to the new popular mood, they need to engage in a fundamental rethinking of capitalism (Jacobs and Mazzucato 2016) guided by better economic theory and a more dynamic relationship between theory and policy.

Unfettered global financial flows are intrinsic to the globalization ideal, but flows collapsed during 2007–09 and nearly ten years later remain well below pre-crisis levels. At their peak, the world's 100 largest banks had a market capitalization of around $4.9 trillion, according to the Bank of England. That was around 8.5 percent of annual global GDP. At its trough, this had fallen to $1.4 trillion, a destruction of the financial capital of $3.5 trillion. The market capitalization of the world's 20 largest banks today remains around half its value in 2007 (Haldane 2016). Since 2008 the G20 economies have become increasingly protectionist. According to the WTO, the advanced economies have, since then, introduced 1,583 new trade restrictions and removed just 387. In a recent report, the WTO noted that between mid-October of 2015 and Mid-May of 2016, G20 countries introduced 145 new protectionist measures, a monthly average of 21, the highest since the WTO began monitoring such measures in 2009 (WTO 2016).

The destabilizing consequences of the crisis and the reversal of the globalization agenda triggered countervailing nationalist and protectionist movements. These should have come as no surprise. First, the financial crisis was a self-inflicted wound. Re-regulation (not de-regulation) of the global economy to favor, detach, and strengthen the rentier (title-holders of money) sector was achieved by deflationary policies. These imposed substantial costs on the real, productive economy where millions expect to be employed, and both enriched and protected the rentier sector from oversight, penalties, and punishment.

References

Elliott, L. (2016). "How America's New President Will Affect the Global." *The Guardian*, November 9, p. 4. Available at: https://www.theguardian.com/business/2016/nov/09/donald-trump-new-us-president-america-global-economy-china-mexico.

Global Network Perspectives (GNP) (2016). "How Will a Trump Presidency Affect Global Business?" *Global Network for Advanced Management*, November. Available at: http://gnp.advancedmanagement.net/article/2016/11/how-will-trump-presidency-affect-global-business.

Haldane, A. G. (2016). "The Great Divide," *BIS Central Bankers' Speeches*, May, p. 22. Available at: https://www.bis.org/review/r160520b.pdf.

Hsu, S. (2017). "Rising U.S. Protectionism May Hurt China's Economy And Begin A Trade War." *Forbes.com*, September.

Jacobs, M. and Mazzucato, M. (2016). "The Brexit-Trump Syndrome: It's the Economics, Stupid." *LSE Blogs*. Available at: https://www.google.com/url?sa=t&rct=j&q=&esrc=s&source=web&cd=2&cad=rja&uact=8&ved=0ahUKEwjZuIaLrM7XAhWJ64MKHUBaA50QFggwMAE&url=http%3A%2F%2Fblogs.lse.ac.uk%2Fpoliticsandpolicy%2Fthe-brexit-trump-syndrome%2F&usg=AOvVaw1s4ANKPIz0KzipgDtgngGn.

Marks, S. and Paravicini, G. (2017). "Brussels to UK: Give Us Clarity on Divorce Bill or Brexit Talks Will Stall." *Politico Magazine*, August.

The Economist (2016). "The Economic Consequences of Donald Trump." November. Available at: https://www.economist.com/blogs/freeexchange/2016/11/global-economy.

Weeks, J. (2016). *Understanding the Corbyn Phenomenon, Dollars and Sense*. Available at: http://dollarsandsense.org/blog/2016/07/understanding-the-corbyn-phenomenon.html.

WTO (2016). *Report on G20 Trade Measures (mid October 2015 to Mid-May 2016)*. Available at: https://www.wto.org/english/news_e/news16_e/g20_wto_report_june16_e.pdf.

WTO (2017). *World Trade Statistical Review*. Available at: https://www.wto.org/english/res_e/statis_e/wts2016_e/wts2016_e.pdf.

Xin, Z. and Yu, X. (2017). "US Businesses May Suffer in Tit-for-Tat Trade War with China, Advisor Says." *South China Morning Post*, March 5. Available at: https://www.cnbc.com/2017/03/05/us-businesses-may-suffer-in-tit-for-tat-trade-war-with-china-advisor-says.html.

14

Disruptive Technologies Driving Growth

Since the dawn of the industrial revolution, technologies have had a disruptive impact on business and society. In the digital age, this impact has become more wide reaching, and the cycle of change has become shorter. The proliferation of technology-based start-ups in the last decade have become significant change agents as new job creators and creators of new business environments. Marginal improvements are creating disruption and new business models by building upon the disruptive power of technology. Think of initiatives like 24/7 online interactive tutoring with subject-matter experts in any part of the world being delivered directly to the consumer and home delivery of goods and services by using a device held in hand from anywhere with little or no human intervention. Marketers are targeting individuals directly through mobile phones which have become an extension of our arm with an average person checking it almost 150 times a day (Willard 2013). These amazing changes are not the beginning and are certainly not the end.

The primary change driver in the current environment has been technology and in today's digital age things are changing even faster. This evolving world is beginning to see a reduction in extreme poverty, an increase in labor standards, greater access to consumer goods, and the facilitation of cultural exchange. In some areas improvement in the cost of living is evident and on a grander scale the stage is set for relative global peace because the criteria for conflict is overpowered by economic parameters.

The Impact of Technology

The impact of technology on the world cannot be overstated. The mere existence of a digital economy and its facilitation of the interconnection of the world with seamless communication and almost instant access to markets make most people over 35 short of breath. This "digitalization" has enabled an increase in international trade while promoting the optimal use of natural resources by countries, allowing them to focus on the production of those goods for which their resources are best suited. Commodities required and not available in the country can be purchased and imported, quite likely at a lower cost. Specialization has encouraged large-scale production and diversity and an optimization of the workforce that is not limited to physical and geographical boundaries. The tendency is also toward stability in terms of pricing products and services around the world as well as the egalitarian effects of globalization. Technological globalization facilitates the exchange of technical know-how and enables formation of new industries in underdeveloped countries by opening up access to machinery and equipment as well as technical expertise that can be imported. This exchange creates increased international competition. Consumers will benefit as producers in these countries produce better quality goods and at the minimum possible cost. As goods move across the world, the natural consequence will be better transport and communication. It has created simplified cooperation and understanding among various groups, an appreciation of other situations, and it encourages an exchange of ideas and cultures. The dramatic changes in the world market and economies have a deleterious effect on old business models. In a constantly changing world, smart leaders are always learning, re-thinking, and re-learning.

The Changing Market Dynamics

Changes in the digital era and the rise of global finance markets has brought both wealth and risk to almost every part of the world. It marks a considerable change from the industrial era. Today's financial markets include Fintech, crowdfunding, and start-up company financing. It has new ways of making payments such as Bitcoins, Apple Pay, and PayPal. The interdependence of global businesses is making global financial markets exhibit more volatility than in the past, which impacts cross-border activity including mergers and acquisition. The shift in the center of gravity of economic power toward Asia and the resulting geopolitics is also impacting capital markets (Quah 2010). In the global economy countries are competing on tax rates to attract businesses to their geographies. The greater "shrinking" of the globe through interconnectedness, increased communication, and awareness of business and investment opportunities makes finance an ever-more important part of the global infrastructure.

Just as technology spawned the traditional business model it is also now its principal disrupter. In the throes of the digital age successful industrial companies are being challenged by a new paradigm. Bookstores are being replaced by Amazon, taxis services are being replaced by Uber, newspapers by social media, and retail stores by e-commerce. Businesses now face a very different set of problems.

The Emergence of the Entrepreneurial Start-up

Technology has changed the playing field by reducing the cost of entry, increasing the speed of access to customers and suppliers, and the scope of the market from local to global. The spread of entrepreneurial start-ups has employed innovation, new products, new strategies, and new ways of doing business that are driving disruption and forcing a large-scale restructuring in the existing corporate structure. The dissemination of technology not only in emerging markets but into every corner of the global market is having a disruptive effect on accepted models.

Technology Driving Growth

The United States has seen economic growth and increasing employment in the past decade from technology companies. Major contributions from companies like Facebook, Twitter, Amazon, Google, and Apple that originated in the late 1990s have blossomed in the last decade. The magnitude of the impact of start-ups can be seen in the US GDP with these major successful start-ups contributing significantly to the GDP of the United States. Technology has created an environment that supported an explosion in start-ups. There is no longer a need for significant investment to support product development. Technology development and even access to venture capital funding can be outsourced through the Internet. Instead of the need to withstand large risks there is a prevalent strategy of taking several small gambles instead of one large bet thereby spreading their risk. The new way to manage business is not a smaller version of a large corporation. It is lean, flexible, open to change, and able to take advantage of the ease with which access is available to global technology and customers within reach. Start-ups' contribution goes beyond money, sound technologies, processes, systems, products, services, and the creation of employment. They are creating a shared economy with jobs and flexibility for everybody by creating an environment of innovation and competition in the market. Silicon Valley, Bangalore, and Tel Aviv are all serving society as innovation city roots (Kola 2014; Compass 2015).

Some would suggest that conversations about inventory systems, smart phones, and communication systems are emblematic of the end of the third phase of the industrial revolution. That statement takes a little unpacking.

The industrial revolution has seen three distinct waves over the past few centuries. The staging of the "pre-industrial society" created environmental, political, and commercial conditions that led to this world-changing ethos that is still in play. The first industrial revolution introduced steam-powered and mechanized production. The second industrial revolution introduced electric power and mass production processes. The third industrial revolution introduced the digitalization of technology. Some currently argue that the fourth industrial revolution has already begun. German economist, Klaus Schwab, declares that "now a Fourth Industrial Revolution is building on the Third, the digital revolution that has been occurring since the end of the last revolution. It is characterised by a fusion of technologies that is blurring the lines between the physical, digital, and biological spheres" (Schwab and Howell 2016).

Technology Connecting Things Around Us

This is the IoT (Internet of Things)—the idea is that there are three stages of IoT development. First, lots of things get connected, including homes, cars, freight trains, medical equipment, and packaged goods. This stage is all about low cost sensors and cheap chips. iBeacons are pieces of plastic costing $5 to $20 that can be as small as an inch square and contain sensors, wireless transceivers, and some memory. They can be stuck in various places and transmit information to devices that pass by them (Ray 2014). Next, more and more analyzable information is extracted from those connected devices. This allows companies to throw together feeds from sensors in the field and combine them with network resources of various kinds. One example is New York Air Brake, a maker of locomotive parts such as valves, hoses, and cylinders. It uses sensor feed to collect and analyze tons of data about vibrations, track conditions, and motion coming from sensors on freight trains. In the final stage, manufacturers run their businesses based on that data thus changing how they earn revenue and learn how to cut costs. Cisco, which has realigned its business to sell packages of switches, software, and services for the IoT, points to the example of a particular application, which is using sensors and networks to gain greater insight into traffic patterns and reduce congestion (Cisco 2017).

We are at the very beginning of this digital world and those things we talk about today as the cutting edge of global business will soon be accepted principles and even be thought of as yesterday's news. The next "blinding flash of the obvious" will be the egalitarian nature of this change. The effect of technology on globalization for multinationals and on local businesses is changing everything. Global businesses must begin to think differently about everything they do.

Innovation Driving Change

Historically, technological empowerment promoted the economic and political climate that is conducive to stability. Water mills, eyeglasses, clocks, and other productivity-enhancing tools put power in the hands of entrepreneurs and merchants in medieval Europe, creating a countervailing economic force against coercive authorities. In response to entrepreneurs' demands and growing economic clout, authorities made compromises, giving rise to important reforms such as property rights, enforcement of contracts, separation of the judiciary from the executive, and other checks and balances, creating the fertile ground needed for economic growth and more egalitarian societies to take root (Morse 2003).

New business models built on the disruptive power of technology can, even with only marginal innovation, create substantial change. There is some truth to the perception that being smarter and thinking "outside of the box" are prerequisites to starting an entrepreneurial venture. However, it is not always accurate. In India, for example, most systems are broken and therein lies opportunity. Take healthcare—despite having world-class doctors and world-class hospitals with the latest equipment from the best manufacturers, India has a system where the basic provision of healthcare still doesn't work properly. The necessary infrastructure to provide basic health services is not adequate. Being super smart or super wealthy is superficial in this conundrum. What is needed is a basic knowledge of the environment and a drive to solve the problems. The catalyst is an entrepreneur that knows the environment, understands the problem, and has a solution. Internet access has enabled an increase in data analysis, mobile phones, smartphones, and the connection of systems that hold viable solutions to legacy problems. One of these creative technological innovations is Portea Medical. In India home healthcare was non-existent before Portea Medical came along. Using the connectivity and capacity of existing technology, they launched a venture based on an entirely different business model providing home healthcare in 22 cities across India with 100,000 home visits a month (Portea 2017). They moved on to address the nutritional aspects of healthcare by creating BigBasket, which provide online grocery purchases with 1 million home deliveries each month across 16 cities. What they have done is not glamorous, it is simply figuring out a solution to deliver eggs, milk, bread, and healthcare directly to homes (Basket 2016).

Iqbal Quadir is best known as the founder of GrameenPhone, now Bangladesh's largest phone company in terms of subscribers. Quadir stitched together a global consortium that launched GrameenPhone in 1997 to provide mobile phone services throughout Bangladesh. His innovative scheme has allowed local entrepreneurs, mostly women, to buy cellular handsets with loans from microcredit pioneer Grameen Bank and then rent the phones, with airtime, to neighbors. Today, GrameenPhone has nearly 1 million direct subscribers, in addition to the 30,000 entrepreneurs whose handsets provide phone access to 50 million people (Morse 2003).

Technology Development Helping to Create New Business Models

The step-by-step development of digital technology from computer, to personal computer, to Internet, worldwide web, laptops, cell phones, smartphones, etc. has represented a tectonic shift in opportunity and has begun a dramatic revision of the business model. Whether by gradual development or exponential leap, these advances have leveled the playing field and given tremendous opportunities to entrepreneurs, as well as spawning the emergence of businesses built on the new model. They are truly disruptive.

The online tutoring company TutorVista, for example, is an amazing success story where serial entrepreneur, India K Ganesh's idea came from a cartoon in a US newspaper. The cartoon basically depicted an American father telling his daughter, "no, you cannot outsource your homework to India." It was meant to be a joke but Ganesh came up with the idea of providing online tutoring that can help students from India or anywhere in the world with their homework.

In today's world the average person checks their mobile phone almost 150 times daily (Willard 2013). Mobile phones have become an extension of our arms. This provides ever-increasing marketing opportunities to targeting individuals directly. With the ability to engage with the consumer directly, comes the ability to sell products and services without employing a message carrier like a radio, television, or mass media with its competition for attention and larger budgets. Again, the character of the technology is disruptive. Mobile phones are always on. Before we get out of bed in the morning, we are checking our phone for messages, emails, and information. We take our phone, tablet, or pad with us everywhere. These devices have geolocation which means we know where we are all the time and so does everyone else. In addition devices are getting smarter. Today's smartphone has approximately the same computing power of a supercomputer ten to 15 years ago, plus a camera, sensors, and more.

Rapidly Changing World of Business

Businesses today have a very different set of problems. First, they need to recognize that today's world is different and old strategies do not apply. For example, connectivity has made the cost of entry of new businesses considerably lower. Smartphones and internet mobility have made it easy to reach customers and suppliers. The competition is not confined to any specific market or geographic boundaries. All of this has meant that businesses must reinvent themselves and play the game by new rules. The skill sets required to earn a living have completely changed. The skills that we have taken for granted no longer exists. Jobs like call center workers, receptionists, air travel check-in, boarding passes, security checks have disappeared. Developments in automation, three-dimensional printing, and the use of robotics in manufacturing, service, medicine, and retail highlight how the nature of employment and the relevant skills needed have changed radically and will continue to do so. The disruption sends its waves crashing into many sectors, and not only in terms of the job itself, but also the ways in which we get the job or the way we get training to build the skills necessary for the job or to stay relevant in the job. Online learning, webinars, and interactive video sessions are expanding, enhancing, and in some cases replacing conventional methods of education. The amount of learning needed to stay relevant, enable performance, and keep a job will continuously change. If you're not learning, you're lagging.

We see these new jobs, new skills, and dynamic of the new business models having both a positive and a negative effect. Demographics become emblematic of a population that has embraced the new paradigm and those that, by intent or happenstance, have not. This demographic dividend provides opportunities for trained able-bodied or able-minded people to move into the workforce. On the flipside this dividend can become a demographic disaster. When young qualified or unqualified populations cannot find work or an outlet for their energy it may lead to anarchy problems. If the traditional sectors, the brick-and-mortar economies hanging on to old sector business models, are not creating enough jobs, there is always a risk of unrest.

Impact of Start-ups

Data tell us that start-ups provide an environment of innovation and competition in the market, which is good for the consumer. This brings a dynamism into the economy that is becoming evident globally. We see innovative technological clusters in places like Tel Aviv, Bangalore, and Silicon Valley. This phenomenon has the potential for advantage in developing economies as well as helping developed ones. Statistics show that US economic growth and increasing employment in the past few decades has come from new technology companies (Compass 2015). Some of them have been new businesses like Instagram, Twitter, Facebook, Amazon, and Groupon, which are not conventional industries but more disruptive innovators that have contributed significantly to the US GDP. When BigBasket, in India, started as an e-grocery company it was truly a technological company, however employment roles included drivers, delivery people, pick-up people, farmers, and employees at the wholesale level to make sure products move to sale. In the Portea Medical start-up, after two and a half years, the company had several thousand employees and not one of them was employed by a hospital.

These start-ups are lean, flexible, and dynamic problem solvers that are also cutting-edge creators. Because of technology, global environments are ripe for the "start-up" culture. The barrier to entry and the effort required is low. With the luxury of learning while they are leaping, they can make mistakes, correct them, and keep right on going. Start-ups are usually organizationally flat and flexible. In the traditional start-up model it could take 12 months or more to launch a company. It involved establishing a full organizational structure that needed to be complete before starting. In the new architecture a couple of people can develop an application, publish it, examine the feedback, and iteratively develop the product. This is a fundamentally different model than the formerly accepted traditional approach. The concept of "on-demand" allows access at the time that consumers want and at the place that they want rather than being constrained by boundaries of time or geography. That has completely changed the development process. This is the flexibility that people want today and the environment in which start-up ventures spawn.

On the macroeconomic side the disruptions in technology or business help new players gain an advantage on a more level playing field. In places like India, with its abundance of technology talent, programming, and computer skills, new technology players have an advantage in creating solutions. In a larger market, again like India, where consumers are extremely price conscious, the purchase power parity is low, and dollar–rupee exchange rate variance is high, it forces development of solutions that are extremely affordable and a good fit for the local market. India is a complex country with multiple languages, cultures, climatic conditions, infrastructures, and challenges. A start-up from India's stress test will be applicable almost anywhere in the world. In countries like Denmark or Singapore, where the markets are small, it forces start-ups to develop different solutions for different countries. Bangalore, with its 12 million people, develops a local solution that is applicable as a quick low-cost opportunity for the entire world. This is particularly the case in core sectors like technology, healthcare, finance, education, media, and entertainment. This technology-driven disruption is still only a scratch on the surface. Advances in data analytics and the Internet of Things, with its new ways of collecting, analyzing, and applying technologies, are changing the world forever.

References

Basket, B. (2016). *Big Basket, Big Basket*. Available at: https://www.bigbasket.com/.

Cisco (2017). *Cisco IoT Networking*. Available at: https://www.cisco.com/c/dam/en/us/products/collateral/se/internet-of-things/brochure-c02-734481.pdf.

Compass (2015). *The Global Startup Ecosystem Ranking 2015*. Available at: http://deep.wylinka.org.br/wp-content/uploads/2015/08/Global-startup-ecosystem-ranking-2015.pdf.

Kola, V. (2014). "Impact of Startups and the Importance of Their Socio-economic Contributions." *Your Story*. Available at: http://yourstory.com/2014/11/impact-of-startups/.

Morse, G. (2003). "Bottom-Up Economics." *Harvard Business Review*, 18–20.

Portea (2017). "Portea—Healing at Home." *Portea*. Available at: https://www.portea.com/about-us/.

Quah, D. (2010). *The Global Economy's Shifting Centre of Gravity*. Available at: http://citeseerx.ist.psu.edu/viewdoc/download?doi=10.1.1.186.1836&rep=rep1&type=pdf.

Ray, T. (2014). "Tech Outlook: The Next Industrial Revolution." *Barron's*. Available at: https://www.barrons.com/articles/tech-outlook-the-next-industrial-revolution-1413002738.

Schwab, K. and Howell, W. L. (2016). *Mastering the Fourth Industrial Revolution*. Geneva. Available at: http://www3.weforum.org/docs/WEF_AM16_Report.pdf.

Willard, S. (2013). "Study: People Check Their Cell Phones Every Six Minutes, 150 Times A Day." *Elite Daily*. Available at: https://www.elitedaily.com/news/world/study-people-check-cell-phones-minutes-150-times-day.

15

Lifestyle Innovations Generating New Businesses

One innovation can drive multiple global businesses. Imagine this situation—you come home after a hard day at work, and the music of your choice starts playing, your digitally enabled refrigerator indicates where the food and drink of your choice are located in the fridge, and recommends what you might like to drink and eat. When you settle down the music identified for your mood comes on automatically. You may be upset because you had to sit in traffic for a while on your way home. The spatial phase imaging technology at your house recognizes your mood based on a comparison with your past behaviors, facial reactions, and compares these with the last time you were in this mood and suggested something to calm you down. All this happens through a standard security camera installed in your own home with and an innovation add-on from Photon-X that makes every pixel on your camera see three dimensions. The same technology can identify the anti-social elements in a crowd, enhance security at any public event venue, and allow your doctor to see under your skin without intrusion. This life-altering technology is not only improving our lifestyle but also creating new business models.

An Innovative Company Helping to Improve our Lifestyle

Photon-X is an innovative company that has developed a new groundbreaking technology for optic sensors—passive spatial phase imaging techniques. Put simply, this technology is an application that allows a camera to see in three dimensions. This is not the development of three-dimensional cameras but an application of three-dimensional technology to regular cameras. Photon-X is focused on driving the sensor technology and software analytics for many different applications. They are used in medicine, security, industry, oil and gas production, entertainment, and even consumer goods. The photonics technology called spatial phase imaging uses silicon technology to look at how light interacts with surfaces. The technology is being built into sensor applications, which will make it extremely cheap and inexpensive to develop. The technology uses a single aperture lens for application anywhere from an endoscope to a telescope to microscopes. The technology has the potential to replace the standard camera or video camera and get to where all three-dimensional technology has always hoped to be. It will be on the chip in the device (PhotonX 2017).

Oil and Gas

Existing applications of this spatial imaging in oil and gas are emblematic of what the future holds. Because these cameras see in such high three-dimensional resolution using a regular or long distance lens pipeline inspection, technology has leapfrogged. Spatial imaging cameras can examine a pipeline a hundred feet away or large oil devices in the middle of the ocean. They can look down the length of a pipe and inspect them to all International Organization for Standardisation (ISO) standards automatically while looking at multiple ISOs' visual inspection criteria. The procedure enables not only inspection but also maintenance all to be done quickly. This allows a significant increase in the number and frequency of inspections. Oil and gas pipelines characteristically traverse rough terrain onshore and offshore yet these devices see little difference. Cameras carried by drones or robotics can inspect pipelines for any type of surface degradation or material loss from inside or outside the pipe and from several hundred miles away. Where there are areas that need to be repaired, it enables preventive maintenance that helps to avoid potential adverse events. Offshore, a camera mounted on a drone can inspect devices under the water. Doing this has been difficult for most sensors because of the strong reflection from the water's surface. Spatial imaging can see through the reflection and provide sharp resolution below the water.

Smart Homes

Applications of this technology seem to be endless. Research into applications for smart homes, smart cities, and smart highway applications begin to unveil the potential impact of IoT (Internet of Things). Spatial imaging brings additional capability for connecting sensors together in smart ways. Much initial research over the years on sound technology, listening to understanding, and responding to voices to enhance human interaction, is being supplemented by adding vision capability. The visual capacity enables detection on analysis to assess movement, patterns, likes and dislikes, detect mood, and more. Because it collects data on everything it can combine elements and anticipate what action to expect. If it is the right time of day, the smart home might recognize from your body language or subtle facial muscle changes that you are hungry and tell you what is in the refrigerator, suggest what you might find appetizing, how you might combine items to make a meal, and maybe even provide a recipe for dinner. It could turn on the oven, order groceries, call the pizza place, count up the calories that were consumed, and suggest a time for a little exercise. If you are not happy with the suggestions it will know because the "gaze" technology has the capability to recognize and respond your emotional state and suggest you should sit down because of your elevated heart rate.

Medical

Application in medicine is probably one of the largest opportunities. The potential of adding new vision for doctors, surgeons, clinicians, and nurses will expand capabilities enabling better decisions and processes. For example, think about a camera that goes behind a conventional endoscope allowing a look inside the body through a small hole. Endoscopic technology has been around for years using regular cameras but the addition of three-dimensional capability that can detect different polyps, their different sizes and shapes, measure them, and also look at the tissue density, is a significant enhancement. The innovation is applicable in multiple medical areas. The real time view of a foreign growth, tissue density, blood vessels, blood flow, etc. are changing what and when detection occurs and provides information that can greatly enhance diagnosis and treatment.

A three-dimensional tablet system is in development that would integrate three-dimensional sensors into Android or iPhone tablets. This would allow medical intervention for wound care, diabetic ulcers, bedsores, and many more ailments. The injury could be quickly uploaded into the cloud enabling viewing by a doctor to see and understand the damage and prescribe appropriate care management. The tablet would allow the physician to have information about the wound size, measure oxygen, or go even deeper and see a number of bacteria, at the site or the formation of heat pockets, tunneling, or abnormal occurrence underneath the skin. Greater understanding of the problem facilitates better and faster healing.

There are also robotic surgery applications allowing actual volumetric area reading that informs decisions on exactly where and how much to cut. Special imaging is moving into developing applications to enhance eye–hand coordination. In robotic surgery, the robot is guided by the surgeon's hand no matter where the surgeon is and with the assistance of imaging the surgical field will be enhanced creating more effective and efficient performance. Because of the ability to assess emotional state the application for pain management will allow for better treatment by enabling better monitoring and more accurate application of pain medication.

Security

The security applications of special imaging are most likely to have the largest immediate potential for impact on moving toward a safer world. The integration of this innovation drives monitoring to a much deeper level than exists today. Most security monitors are nothing more than video cameras that are placed almost everywhere, connected to hundreds of monitors that typically are in arrays of maybe ten monitors with observers sitting viewing as best they can. There exists a phenomenon called monitor blindness. This is a physical condition afflicting observers which means they simply miss what is happening even though it flashes before their eyes. Hence the development of intelligent video inspection that automates the process. For example, if someone walks into a room the system uses biometric applications to identify them. It will detect where they are in the room, and if they have a package, it can detect what they do with it.

"Volumetric bounding box" technology allows analytics that enable an understanding of events taking place. Based on the data, it can predict likely occurrences within the context of the setting. Beyond just prediction, it can also track indicators such as, has a package been set down and how far away is the owner? It can enhance or flag the package based on its situation; that is, is the owner present, five feet away, or has it been abandoned? This new intelligence will not only provide better prevention security but in the case of actual events, enable better response by first responders. This has secure environment application in airports, hospitals, movie theaters, and elsewhere.

Other innovations that are adding capability to security are the biometrics application tools that detect faces from a distance. Three-dimensional facial recognition is possible from hundreds of feet away. With the right lens technology it is possible to read emotions from long distances and predict potential outcomes. New spatial phase imaging technology that sees, records, and understands the three-dimensional flow of data is not just data collection, it is three-dimensional analytics and understanding of what's happening with surface changes. For instance, it is possible to actually read how a face is changing over time, which muscles are actually moving. This involves not hundreds but millions of pixel size changes on a face. The system knows every surface muscle that changes and correlates those to emotional states extremely accurately. Also, technology can read the fingerprints of someone from a distance greater than the 15 feet, which is the case currently. Iris detection, iris recognition, and eye gazing applications also add to the ability to provide pertinent information sooner and of better quality.

Manufacturing and Logistics

Some huge strides have been made in the creation of automated manufacturing tools that help manufacturers. One application recognizes what is being looked at and how it is assembling, and does so in a single area and on a single platform. For example, developing tools will look at a volumetric box of almost any size. Within that volumetric area it will record and measure precisely anything that's within the field to within three-thousandths of an inch. This allows a person, or robot, to maneuver within that area, whether it is to have a robot drill a hole at some specific angle and orientation or to move material from one place to the other. It will guide that robot to the correct location and provide volumetric analysis on manufacturing and assembling objects within that field. This changes the large manufacturing assembly lines model by making one-location operations more advantageous and less expensive while changing the paradigm of the industry. Everything happens in one place and one setting. Smart robots will be able to intelligently and with precision, manufacture and assemble within one volumetric space at a single location. This adds capacity, decreases the size of manufacturing facilities, increases efficiency and performance of manufacturing settings, and drives toward a future autonomous manufacturing capability. This will of course have a corresponding effect on logistics, with diminished demand for the movement of parts and the finished product from other locations.

Education

This three-dimensional capability, allowing for the recognition of emotions, has dramatic applications in education too. It will move education away from the classroom or at least, change the definition of the classroom. The increasingly complicated nature of the world dictates that students will be demanding highly specialized education processes that don't fit well with old school thinking. Spatial imaging with its recognition and analytic capacities will be able to use old and new accepted tools to deliver a highly specialized and individualized curriculum. The technology will monitor student response and tailor the learning process based on how the learner learns. It will use all the nuances of the innovation to facilitate the best presentation of the appropriate educational process and content. We can already see some of this potential operating in today's world. The commercial availability of virtual reality and augmented reality in gaming applications could have a far-reaching impact on education. Even the concept of gaming as a learning tool will soon be a recog nized instrument of education just as university curriculums offer gaming as an educational option today.

We stand, yet again, on the brink of significant technological innovations that were unthinkable only a decade ago. With the recognition that technology growth fuels more technology growth, today's innovations, as astounding as they appear, are only the beginning. Imagine how many global businesses will be born from this continuing technology evolution.

Reference

PhotonX (2017). "Photon X Technology." *Photon-X*. Available at: http://www.photon-x.com/.

16

Analytics Taming the Data Monster

In this digital world in two days we create as much information as we did from the beginning of time until 2003. In addition that cycle replicates every two days (Siegler 2010). The volume of data being captured and stored is mind boggling. Every minute more than 210 million emails are generated, 2 million Facebook posts, 300,000 tweets, 200,000 photos are uploaded to Facebook, and 575 new websites are viewed (Bernardmarr 2014). It seems that there is quantum disruption coming in the decision-making process in the way massive amounts of data and its analysis is being used to make decisions. Data about personal choices are collected at every interaction point, and data location flows through the daily use of mobile devices, and these are being used by companies for making business choices. It may seem that those who are in control of data may know more about the person than the person himself, however, if you look at Brexit and the US elections, data analytics pretty much failed to deliver significant insight.

In Chapter 14, Disruptive Technologies Driving Growth, a view of technology is presented from the broader perceptive of where we have been in the past 150 years.

> The staging of the "pre-industrial society" created environmental, political, and commercial conditions that led to this world-changing ethos that is still in play. The first industrial revolution introduced steam-powered and mechanized production. The second industrial revolution introduced electric power and mass-production processes. The third industrial revolution introduced the digitalization of technology. Some currently argue that the fourth industrial revolution has already begun. German economist, Klaus Schwab, declares that "now a Fourth Industrial Revolution is building on the Third, the digital revolution that has been occurring since the end of the last revolution". It is characterised by a fusion of technologies that is blurring the lines between the physical, digital, and biological spheres" (Schwab and Howell 2016).

This fourth revolution is revealing its presence and relevance to global business in tangible ways. The Internet of Things (IoT) refers to the connection of devices to the Internet. These are not "old school" devices like computers and smartphones. Lots of things get connected including homes, cars, freight trains, medical equipment, packaged goods, and the human body. These sensor chips are small, inexpensive, simple, and powerful. Each chip contains sensors, wireless transceivers, and some memory. They collect data and pass it on without any human interaction or intervention. IoT enables the capture of mountains of data. The data itself, though titillating to think about, is useless if there is no system to sort it and ferret out what it is telling us. Thus the arrival of data mining and the growing trends in start-up businesses are focusing on software to parse and analyze the mounds of information. Also, businesses are beginning to realize the value to be derived and applied in the pursuit of higher performance and efficiencies. In other words, the field of analytics is hot.

Why do we Need Data Analytics?

Analytics is about making good business decisions. Just getting reports with numbers does not help. Information must be presented in a way that best suits decision-makers. Data should not replace common sense or experience but is swiftly becoming an irreplaceable strategic weapon in the business world especially. Competitive advantage is data-driven. As the world evolves, the ability to leverage data's story is essential. Analytics is different from analysis. It is multidisciplinary with extensive application of mathematics and statistics. It is not so much concerned with individual analyses or analysis steps as a methodology that relies on the simultaneous application of statistics, computer programming, and operations research to quantify performance.

Intuition and Data

Most decision-making models, including statistical models, have some element of intuition in them. There is a value to the human experience and capacity to think creatively about applications of varied sources of information. This is the model used by business over the centuries and has yielded a wide range of outcomes based on the human factor. Good thinkers and savvy leaders tend to make better decisions but there is no guarantee of that. Though it is a fine art, it lacks the specificity of science. It has been the accepted paradigm for so long leadership may find it challenging to adopt other perspectives or appreciate the idea of intuition and add a more scientific methodology that is less volatile. The idea of using analytics is a disruptor that will facilitate change applying different rules to old systems. Leaders in business are recognizing that intuition connected to innovation coming out of consumer analytics provides new insight into what consumers want. Those answers, which business has been guessing, are leveraged from the data captured at the transaction level. We can learn from customers and see exactly what they want even before they know they want it. That is a strategic edge that will make its way into leadership thinking and will become the new paradigm.

Data-driven Decision Making

Even though corporate leaders may not be data scientists, the change is evident inside organizations with data analysts that are developing a better understanding of the business or a particular department from a real world perspective. This new "breed" has a greater recognition of how the data drive good decisions. US Bureau of Labor Statistics has reported that the job market for data analysts is growing at almost 30 percent annually. This is three times more than the national job growth average of around 10 percent (BLS 2017). This is an indication of demand driven by the realization of the importance of analytics and how it will impact almost everything. There is a high demand for analytics and urgency for businesses to move swiftly. There is an ever increasing need for perfecting the analytics of the data and an expanded opportunity for innovation. Universities are increasingly offering specialized degree programs on analytics. Demand for the training is growing with the salaries of data analysts reflecting the supply and informing the market.

Is it an Art or a Science?

Qualitative and quantitative features of the demand are important to examine. Quantitatively there is a lot of data and a real need for people who can understand, analyze, and strategize around it. Qualitatively there is a move away from the intuition-based analysts to the recognition of the untold and undiscovered story from the data. There is an acknowledgment of the need to discover the "hidden secrets" of a particular domain. The explosion of information is driving more qualitative performance. Someone who is an expert in one area, with a vast understanding of the limited data available, can unzip the storehouse of information waiting, inside the existing data, driving the creation of innovation. As the innovation continues, we see moves toward more automation and artificial intelligence that enable an even deeper dive into the data. While the engineering of analytics is a science, there still exists the need for the art of analytics. It is the art and science working together which produce quality deliverables. The concept is moving from the analyst's office into every other part of the business from operation, to finance, to human relations, to the executive offices.

Need of the Hour

The pressure on information technology is continuing to create technologies that provide accurate, concise, tailored, and immediate answers to data bound questions. This is one of the most challenging and brightest opportunities in the field as businesses move into the future. There is a shortage of talent in strategy, core development, technology, and engineering. The strategy is the art and the fascinating piece of developing and maintaining a competitive edge. Leaders traditionally have the strongest sense of the pulse of business because of their connection to the culture or strategic sense. However, with the evolution of engineering and its importance in the science of business, the leader's job increasingly becomes preserving and protecting the company culture. In a world of many emails per minute, leaders must stay calm and composed and understand how quickly the situation can change. They must move faster than their competitors and get new information and changes embedded into the corporate culture.

A company that builds heavy engineering benches and sells to the military might benefit on many levels from discovering the analytics of their bench and strategizing its improvement. A modem manufacturer selling to heavy equipment manufacturers enabling them to capture and analyze data on fuel consumption, location, load, and other efficiencies will drive higher performance. Both of these examples are based on progressive leaders who are willing to embrace change, even contrary to the accepted paradigms, in order to remain competitive. Analytics helps leaders to structure their thinking, expand options, innovate strategies, implement initiatives, and facilitate change.

There is certainly a shortage of time, talent, and technology with a countervailing demand for analytics. The media has done an extraordinary job of creating business panic resulting in some businesses jumping in early. Despite this there is much room for improvement and a vast opportunity for all businesses. For local businesses it is easier. They are usually singularly focused on a well-defined value chain, delivery channels, well-designed site, a unique presence, and minimal sources. Global firms have a massive cultural, social, and economic impact to consider. In their case analytics are critical. Dealing with a parameter that the taste of mango changes every 250 miles, to a business dealing in mangoes this is a relatively important fact. It means that to fully serve a market, like Asia, some consideration must be given to the approximately 270 flavors of mango in that market. The power of analytics to capture and analyze data at the pallet level can be the difference between selling mango and going home.

Helping to Make the Best Decision

One of the primary elements of sales success in a retail business is pricing strategy. Product pricing is consumer based on an understanding of a product's value to the consumer. Analytics can track change at the consumer level related to a particular business line and, in a matter of an hour, predict what the consumer wants and what their appetite for purchase is at different price points. Compared to a competitor without such tools, the same decision-making process could take four days. Another example is oil drilling companies using seismic data to figure out where to drill. If they end up digging the wrong hole it is a colossal failure and lost investment. Analytics is helping to shape that part of the industry in substantial ways. Pinpointing the place to drill the well is dramatically reducing the risk of dry wells and dramatically increasing profitability. That is a competitive advantage. That is the power of analytics.

Data Gathering from Mobiles

Today, we live in a world of mobile devices, and these devices have provided access to location specific information. The mobile device can tell companies about our taste, preferences of our movement, food, and anything else. This is geospatial analytics. 23 percent of the organizations today are using location intelligence (Levy 2015). They are predicting who is visiting points of sale and where a product will sell. The geospatial analytics have been mainstream for several years. Data analysts will move beyond collecting location data from connected devices, combining it with other information, and conducting a deep analysis on the spot. The decreasing cost of iBeacons that collect and forward data will enable its presence in more locations. iBeacons in stores to detect when people enter and where they spend time and money, enable a better understanding of merchandise, and the personalization of merchandising. The transportation industry expands its use of data from connected cars and automated public transport systems to reduce congestion and emissions. Manufacturing operations increase the connectivity of machines which improve operations and predict maintenance needs. Some would say there is quantum disruption coming in the way factories are run, business decisions and personal choices are made, and the way the world works.

Balancing the Art and the Science

This prevalence and analyses of data implies an enormous cultural element of trust. Understanding and respecting the relation between trust and privacy and the importance of the human element is paramount. Data itself means nothing. It is the value that data delivers that carries the interest. Science is predictable. Science is what we know. Art is the interpretation of what we know and must be preserved. Art is what defines us, it is our core, the differentiator. Losing the art results in the online retail store, during summer, suddenly noticed a huge spike in demand for holiday ornaments and having no clue why. Despite that they started acting on that information and building their inventory of ornaments. However, it was summer so the costs were higher because it was not the season for ornaments and they had to revive their supply chain and order a special production run. After some digging they discovered that their system had filled in a seasonal item that was temporarily popular as a free shipping option that customers had not filled in. The system itself was adjusting by using an ornament to fill up that gap. This is science played with no art. The lesson is that there needs to be a balance of art and science. The data is meaningless without the application of cognizant art. Jim Collins, in his book *Good to Great*, tells the story of Admiral Stockdale who was captured in the Vietnam War. He asked who would die first. He said the optimists would die first because when their hopes were shattered around them they would not survive. Next to die would be the pessimists because they were just killing themselves anyway. The only ones to survive would be the realists because they understood the situation. They understood both optimism and the pessimism and had long ago decided they could survive on the middle ground (Collins 2001).

There is evidence of the presence of dehumanized analytics. It must be understood that data is only as good as its source. Missing out on the origin of data skews the value of the analytics. Without context it will not tell the truth. It is incumbent for businesses to understand the source of the data and to include as many sources as possible because the more you know, the more you learn and the better the outcome. This new paradigm is not about building a culture around analytics, it is about analytics empowering the culture.

References

Bernardmarr (2014). *Big Data: 25 Amazing Need-to-Know Facts, SmartDataCollective.* Available at: https://www.smartdatacollective.com/big-data-25-facts-everyone-needs-know/.

BLS (2017). *Employment Situation Summary.* Available at: https://www.bls.gov/news.release/empsit.nr0.htm.

Collins, J. (2001). *Good to Great and the Social Sectors: Why Business Thinking is Not the Answer*. USA: Harper Collins.

Levy, H. P. (2015). *Add Location to Your Analytics, Smarter With Gartner*. Available at: https://www.gartner.com/smarterwithgartner/add-location-to-your-analytics/.

Schwab, K. and Howell, W. L. (2016). *Mastering the Fourth Industrial Revolution*. Geneva: Garter. Available at: http://www3.weforum.org/docs/WEF_AM16_Report.pdf.

Siegler, M. (2010). "Eric Schmidt: Every 2 Days We Create As Much Information As We Did Up To 2003." *Techcrunch*. Available at: https://techcrunch.com/2010/08/04/schmidt-data/.

Part IV
The World Tomorrow

17

The Future of Work and the Changing Workplace

The world of work has been impacted by technology. Work is different now than it was in the past due to digital innovation. Labor market opportunities are becoming polarized between high-end and low-end skilled jobs. Migration and its effects on employment have become a sensitive political issue. From Buffalo to Beijing public debates are raging about the future of work. Development in automation like artificial intelligence and machine intelligence are contributing to productivity, efficiency, safety, and convenience but are also having an impact on jobs, skills, wages, and the nature of work. The "undiscovered country" of the workplace today is the combination of the changing landscape of work itself and the availability of ill-fitting tools, platforms, and knowledge to train for the requirements, skills, and structure of this new age.

The Change

The work landscape is rapidly evolving. A new generation of workers is beginning to fill the labor force. This is a generation born into the age of technology and challenging conventional ideas of work. Businesses are struggling to adapt to employees' new perceptions with a widening gap between the skills employers need from their workers and the workers that are available. Employers face the challenge of how to educate tomorrow's workforce and are realizing that the tools they have available to them are from the past. The Society for Human Resource Management (SHRM), is one of the leading research organizations in human resources. They recently published the list of greatest challenges for today's businesses and at the top of that list was the skill gap. It highlighted how educational institutes are producing the future workforce with tools that industry no longer requires. Businesses are having a hard time in coping with the technological revolution and in some instances technology itself is obsolete. The challenge is how businesses can obtain this workforce for the future when the environment and the business itself are not equipped to prepare them.

The workplace is also experiencing a decreasing sense of loyalty from their workers. At one point it was not uncommon to have a worker remain in one job for their entire career. As technologies increase, that longevity has decreased to ten years, then seven, five, and now in the millennials' era it is down to three years. Businesses typically take about a year to prepare an employee to be an integral productive part of the team. This means the businesses are not equipping employees inside and people are not getting trained outside. Unlike their grandparents or even their parents, millennials are not likely to stay with one employer for their entire career. In fact, by the time they hit 30, some so-called GenY workers already have experience with several companies under their belt. That means companies have to work harder to retain young workers, often offering lifestyle perks that were not on the table years ago. Moreover, for workers, it means more flexibility; you no longer have to stick it out at a job for three years if the company is not right for you. It also means companies have to use new approaches to entice these workers. Both in terms of when you work and where you work, more companies are offering—and more employees are asking for—workplace flexibility. Because the workplace has gone digital, employees based in an office can often take their work on the road, which provides opportunities to live closer to family, relocate to a new city, travel, or simply work from home in their pyjamas. The question is whether their employere embrace this new trend.

Generation Effect

This new workforce views work differently than their predecessors. The average US worker spends 25 percent of the day reading and answering emails. The average mobile phone user checks their device 150 times a day and 60 percent chatted at least once every hour (Daily Mail 2013). Maybe because GenY watched their parents work their lives away, the workplace's newer employees want time to develop their personal lives and interests outside of work. They also want the work itself to be fulfilling, not just to provide a paycheck. Employers trying to compete for talent are meeting these demands in creative ways, offering at-work perks like food and laundry services or giving workers the option of a sabbatical. 40 percent of the US population believes it is impossible to succeed at work and have a balanced family life. This labor force is bound for employment at companies of which 80 percent rate their business as highly complex or complex for employees. Fewer than 16 percent of companies have programs to simplify work or help employees deal with stress. The average US worker works 47 hours per week, 49 percent work for 50 hours or more per week, and 20 percent work for 60+ hours per week (Isidore and Luhby 2015). The mismatch between what the corporate workplace offers and what the new workforce wants is hard to miss.

Old Jobs are Gone

The former US President Barack Obama commented on these changes by saying we should not be waiting for the jobs that have disappeared in the past but should be preparing the workforce for jobs that are coming in the future. The old jobs are most likely gone forever. Long-term unemployment could be here to stay. Long-term joblessness has become a fixture of our economy, so much so that some workforce experts worry the class might become permanent. About 6.2 million people have been jobless for more than six months, the benchmark for long-term unemployment, according to the US Labor Department's July jobs report (BLS 2017). That group accounts for about 44 percent of the unemployed.

The New Work Environment

The new workforce does not wear its technology like the old one; it lives it. Technology is part of who they are. They choose to work from anywhere at any time and they do not long for the uniformity of the old work style and the old workplace. If you look in the business section of any bookshop you'll find dozens of titles promising to share the secret to climbing the corporate ladder. However, the day is not far off when such books will seem as quaint and outmoded as a housekeeping manual from the 1950s. Key workplace trends of the twenty-first century have seen the collapse of the corporate ladder, whereby loyal employees climbed towards the higher echelons of management one promotion at a time. Cathy Benko, vice chairman of Deloitte in San Francisco and co-author of *The Corporate Lattice*, says that the ladder model dates back to the industrial revolution when successful businesses were built on economies of scale, standardization, and a strict hierarchy (Benko 2010). "But we do not live in an industrial age, we live in a digital age. Moreover, if you look at all the shifts taking place, one [of the biggest] is the composition of the workforce, which is far more diverse in every way," she says.

This new diversity, combined with technological advances, has fed demand for a more collaborative and flexible working environment. Benko estimates that companies have "flattened out" by about 25 percent over the past 25 years, losing several layers of management in favor of a more grid-like structure, where ideas flow along horizontal, vertical, and diagonal paths. Career paths are becoming similarly fluid, with many following a zigzag rather than a straight path. "I would argue that [the lattice model] provides more opportunity and more possibilities to be successful," says Benko. "In the ladder model, you are looking in one direction, which is up. In the lattice organisation you can find growth by doing different roles, so you have new experiences, you acquire new skills, you tap into new networks. The world is less predictable than it was in the industrial age, so you stay relevant by acquiring a portfolio of transferable skills" (Benko 2010).

The Impact of Start-ups

More people are working for themselves. Entrepreneurship is hot, partly because start-ups like Facebook have gained notoriety, and partly because the recession left some workers with no other options. More people became self-employed in 2010 than during each of the past 15 years, according to a report from the Ewing Marion Kauffman Foundation, a think tank that focuses on entrepreneurship (Fairlie et al. 2015). However, most entrepreneurs work on their own, without hiring other workers, which means they are not creating a significant number of jobs for the economy. Personal branding is all the rage. Online branding of individuals is affecting industries across the board, as well as the job search process. Making a name for yourself is smarter than ever in this volatile economy, increasing your chances that someone who knows of you will come to you with a job rather than you having to look for one when you need it. Especially since the newest generation of workers tend to hop from one company to another, it makes sense to brand yourself rather than (or in addition to) your employer.

Trends

A study from McKinsey said that the most disruptive trends that businesses face are in the automation of work. In recent years, automation has become increasingly prevalent. We think nothing of paying for groceries at a scanner or transferring money on a screen without going into a bank. We have grown accustomed to the idea of self-driving cars and computers that can talk to us. As marvellous as these innovations may seem, they can also be destructive, rendering entire professions obsolete even as they boost productivity and convenience. Moreover, now, if widespread predictions are correct, automation in the workplace is set to increase at an unprecedented rate. "There's going to be a huge change, comparable to the industrial revolution," says

Jerry Kaplan, a Silicon Valley entrepreneur who teaches a class in artificial intelligence at Stanford. Robots and intelligent computer systems, he says, "are going to have a far more dramatic impact on the workplace than the internet has" (Fox and O'Connor 2010).

Kaplan is not alone in this belief. A 2013 study by the Oxford Martin School estimated that 47 percent of jobs in the United States could be susceptible to computerization over the next two decades (Frey and Osborne 2013). A study by the McKinsey Global Institute predicted that, by 2025, robots could jeopardize between 40 million and 75 million jobs worldwide (Manyika et al. 2017). "There have been two major developments over the past ten years," says Kaplan. "The first relates to advances in machine learning—the ability to organise large volumes of data so you can get actionable intelligence. The second is the availability of data of all kinds, coming from smartphones and other low-cost sensors out there in the environment. When you add those two things up—the availability of the data along with the ability to interpret it—it enables a whole lot of things that you could not do before."

Capital Replacing Labor

By absorbing the most routine aspects of our jobs, optimists argue, machines are freeing us up to concentrate on more creative, thoughtful activities. This may be true for some, but, as the Silicon Valley entrepreneur and author Martin Ford says: "The reality is that a very large fraction of our workforce is engaged in activities that are on some level routine, repetitive and predictable." If this is the case, retraining a large portion of the workforce to engage in more creative activity beyond the reach of automation will pose an enormous challenge. One issue that will loom ever larger as the incidence of automation increases, according to Kaplan, is inequality. "Automation is fundamentally the substitution of capital for labour. The problem is that the people who already have the capital are the ones who will benefit most because they are the ones who will invest in the new automation" (Manyika et al. 2017).

"I Uploaded the Work"

Websites that match employers with freelancers are growing fast—and so is the potential for lower wages and inequality. In the past decade cloud computing has radically altered the way we work, but it's the growth of the "human cloud," a vast global pool of freelancers who are available to work on demand from remote locations on a mind-boggling array of digital tasks, which is actually set to shake up the world of work (Fox and O'Connor 2010).

The past five years have seen a proliferation of online platforms that match employers (known in cloud-speak as "requesters") with freelancers (often referred to as "taskers"), inviting them to bid for each task. Two of the biggest sites are Amazon's Mechanical Turk, which lays claim to 500,000 "turkers" from 190 countries at any given time, and Upwork, which estimates that it has 10 million freelancers from 180 countries in its database (Williams 2016). They compete for approximately 3 million tasks or projects each year, which can range from tagging photos to writing code. The market is evolving so quickly that it is hard to pin down exactly how many people are using these sites worldwide, but management consultants McKinsey estimate that by 2025 some 540 million workers will have used one of these platforms to find work (Fox and O'Connor 2010).

> The benefits for companies using these sites are obvious: instant access to a pool of cheap, willing talent, without having to go through lengthy recruitment processes. Moreover, no need to pay overheads and holiday or sick pay. For the "taskers" the benefits are less clear cut. Champions of the crowdsourcing model claim that it is a powerful force for the redistribution of wealth, bringing a fresh stream of income and flexible work into emerging economies such as India and the Philippines (two of the biggest markets for these platforms). However, herein lies the problem, as far as critics are concerned. By inviting people to bid for work, sites such as Upwork inevitably trigger a "race to the bottom", with workers in Mumbai or Manila able to undercut their peers in Geneva or London thanks to their lower living costs.   (Fox and O'Connor 2010)

Take Over by Machines

Like it or not, we are in the midst of the fourth industrial revolution. Machines are now negotiating with other machines to increase productivity, machines are moving closer and closer to humans with Fitbits to keep us healthy, Apple watches, SIRI, and Cortana to keep us organized. A study at the Massachusetts Institute of Technology (MIT) estimated it would require roughly 3,000 coordinated cars to take care of 90 percent of New York City's traffic with less than a five-minute wait. That means a company like Uber or Lyft or any cloud collaborative taxi service could efficiently handle New York traffic with just 3,000 cars. This means taking 2.7 million vehicles off the city streets each day, which has enormous consequences, some good and some bad (Smith 2017). The emergence of autonomous vehicles would change the entire ecosystem of drivers and supply chains with technology tectonics bringing about a seismic impact.

This tectonic shift will come quickly but will have long-lasting consequences. It will change the entire fundamental structure of the workplace. "It is a factor in driving down real wages and increasing inequality," says Guy

Standing, professor of economics at SOAS, University of London. He predicts falling wages because workers will be in worldwide competition for jobs. "And it is not just unskilled labour that's being done online," says Standing. "It goes all the way up: legal services, medical diagnosis, architectural services, and accounting—it is affecting the whole spectrum" (Fox and O'Connor 2010).

The Changing Workplace

It is becoming easier than ever for employers to keep an eye on their staff. With emerging technologies, companies can monitor where employees are and what they are up to but also how they are feeling—whether they are stressed, tired, or not getting enough exercise outside work. Some workplace tracking technologies are already widely used. Low-cost GPS systems are used to record the progress of delivery drivers. Earpieces relay orders to warehouse employees and can also track their performance and downtime. At Amazon, workers are encouraged to report on each other's performance via an online feedback tool. There is even an implantable chip that serves as a security card and geo-locator tracking all sorts of data on employees. Why would your employer want to know how much you exercise or how well you're sleeping at night? "Really, it is a management diagnostic tool," says Chris Brauer, Director of Innovations at Goldsmiths, University of London. "What impacts on your performance at work is not just what you do at work. In our early stage studies, we find strong, clear correlations between sleep patterns and concentration, between levels of anxiety and stress outside the workplace and performance inside the workplace" (Forrest 2016). Among various objections to such initiatives, perhaps the strongest has to do with the invasion of privacy.

As people live longer—life expectancy at birth has increased globally by six years since 1990, according to the World Health Organization—they are expected to work longer (Parry 2015). The pressure comes from governments, which struggle to afford pensions for a longer-living population, and also from individuals themselves, who find it harder to make their retirement savings stretch as the average life expectancy rises. These trends have led to speculation that we are approaching the end of retirement or at least entering a period in which older workers will stop working gradually rather than abruptly upon reaching retirement age.

The challenge, as it has been from the dawn of human history, is not what happens but how we handle what happens. This tsunami of technology is relentless and hiding from it or blaming its change on ideology or human malfeasance will do less than putting our finger in the hole in the dyke. The test will be turning it to our advantage as a powerful tool for human advancement.

References

Benko, C. (2010). "How the Corporate Ladder Became the Corporate Lattice." *Harvard Business Review.*

BLS (2017). *Employment Situation Summary.* Available at: https://www.bls.gov/news. release/empsit.nr0.htm.

Daily Mail (2013). "Average Smartphone User Checks It Every Six Minutes—Or 150 Times a Day." Available at: http://www.dailymail.co.uk/news/article-2330851/Your-smartphone-ruining-long-weekend-Average-user-checks-device-minutes–150-times-day.html.

Fairlie, R. W., Reedy, E. J., Morelix, A., and Russell, J. (2015). *The KAUFFMAN INDEX, Stast Up activity National Trends.* Available at: https://www.mckinsey.com/~/media/mckinsey/featured%20insights/Digital%20Disruption/Harnessing%20automation%20for%20a%20future%20that%20works/MGI-A-future-that-works-Executive-summary.ashx

Forrest, A. (2016). "'Assume You're Being Monitored, Because You Probably Are'—The Future of Workplace Surveillance." *VICE.* Available at: https://www.vice.com/en_uk/article/kwxjww/assume-youre-being-monitored-because-you-probably-are-the-future-of-workplace-stalking.

Fox, K. and O'Connor, J. (2010). "Five Ways Work Will Change in the Future." *The Guardian.* Available at: https://www.theguardian.com/society/2015/nov/29/five-ways-work-will-change-future-of-workplace-ai-cloud-retirement-remote.

Frey, C. B. and Osborne, M. A. (2013). *The Future of Employment: How Susceptible Are Jobs To Computerisation?.* Available at: https://www.oxfordmartin.ox.ac.uk/downloads/academic/The_Future_of_Employment.pdf.

Isidore, C. and Luhby, T. (2015). "Turns Out Americans Work Really Hard...But Some Want to Work Harder." *CNN money.* Available at: http://money.cnn.com/2015/07/09/news/economy/americans-work-bush/index.html.

Manyika, J., Chui, M., Miremadi, M., Bughin, J., George, K., Willmott, P., and Dewhurst, M. (2017). *A Future that Works: Automation, Employment, and Productivity.* Available at: file:///C:/Users/mahes/Downloads/MGI-A-future-that-works_Full-report.pdf.

Parry, L. (2015). "Global Life Expectancy Has Risen by 6 Years Since 1990...But We Spend Longer Living with Illness and Disability." *Daily Mail.* Available at: http://www.dailymail.co.uk/health/article-3211548/Global-life-expectancy-risen-6-years-1990.html.

Smith, C. (2017). "MIT: 3,000 Uber and Lyft Cars Could Completely Replace All New York City Taxis." *BGR.* Available at: http://bgr.com/2017/01/03/mit-study-uber-and-lyft/.

Williams, R. (2016). "What Will Happen When Robots Can Do Most Jobs?" *Psychology Today.* Available at: https://www.psychologytoday.com/blog/wired-success/201608/what-will-happen-when-robots-can-do-most-jobs.

18

The Future of Human Workers

Robots, Artificial Intelligence, and Human Beings

New technologies like artificial intelligence, robotics, machine intelligence, and the Internet of Things are seeing repetitive tasks move away from human to machines. Humans cannot become machines, but machines can become more human-like. Today's addition to this continuum is that technology has enhanced the pace of innovation and the need for focused learning in new skill arenas. It has become necessary to avoid becoming irrelevant tomorrow. The normal life cycle of workers has been to consume a lifetime worth of preparation in the first few years of life and for the rest of the time draw down on that depositary. This traditional model is fast becoming irrelevant. Now the model is to learn, work, and enjoy at the same time. This is creating a massive need for the retooling of existing human workers. Another major issue for individuals is the need to train their minds to remain focused in a society which is constantly getting bombarded with information at a frantic pace. It seems like that we may have to become a sort of corporate yogi with the spiritual and mental capacity to start with, unlike a corporate athlete. Corporate athletes began with building physical capacity than emotional and mental capacity and finally the spiritual capacity (Loehr and Schwartz 2001). The two starting factors of physical and mental capacity are slowly being taken away by machines and artificial intelligence. The order of capacity building is almost reversed now with a starting point being to build your spiritual capacity like a yogi to stay away from distractions created by technology in order to build mental and physical capacity.

We discussed in the last chapter how changes in the world have evolved the nature of organizations, the shift in the work environment, and changes in the way work is getting done. The global scope of business driven by technology has challenged existing norms and seen the creation of new paradigms. The new workforce has grown up in this world and views work differently from their predecessors. We also saw how the workforce has forced structural changes in the organization itself. The monolithic corporate model with it stable and loyal lifelong employees is changing into a nimbler structure that shares workers from a pooled workforce. The growth of automation and machine learning is changing the workplace and the workforce with the prediction of the disappearance of millions of jobs. The ever accelerating cycle of accumulated knowledge and the availability and access to vast amounts of data and information have impacted almost every corner of the globe, changing not only how we work but how we live and what we expect. This global world is changing everything and at an ever-increasing speed. This can indeed be a stressful and fearful time for workers and businesses as well. In this chapter, we unpack this dilemma and take a fresh look at it.

The Subtle Transition

Things that have given comfort and stability for generations are experiencing significant changes and are driving how we work and the kind of work environment that we move to in the future. There is a growing need for high-end skills. This puts workers that stay a long time with the same company at a disadvantage because they lose the exposure to newer technologies that might be developing elsewhere in the market. Workers are pressured because of the rate at which technology changes and the need to constantly be renewing and refreshing their skills. Employee learning itself has changed from knowing the entire encyclopaedia to having to understand a single proficiency. In the new marketplace workers will need a little of both. Finally, the demand for low or no skilled jobs is decreasing while demand for high-skilled jobs is increasing. However, until the time that technology takes the next leap forward there is a hidden workforce estimated at several hundreds of million workers that will most likely remain relevant. This hidden workforce is evident in most emerging economies populating the city streets with vendors, taxis, shoe shines, individuals making and selling clothes and food, and housewives sewing and cooking, that is, doing those things that will probably be the last place that technology reaches.

Master-Slave Dynamic

The master-slave dynamic has subtly existed in human culture from our early confrontation with technologies. Let's think of fire as a way making food more digestible by cooking it, or partially pre-digesting it, before consumption and of language that facilitates coordinated efforts between people and technologies.

Both have significantly shaped modern human beings. The creation of money, which is an interesting concept in itself, was meant to enable trading value for value yet in the monetary system value is traded for essentially a piece of paper and potentially just electronic bits and bytes. Money is a new technology that changed the shape and culture of our civilization. As did railways, electricity, digital expertise, and so will artificial intelligence.

It is convenient to believe that we are the masters of our technology and that we can go wherever we want and do whatever we want. However, on examination this may not be true. In today's world, algorithms and technologies are telling us what to read, what to eat, what to wear, and what to do. We are co-evolving with these technologies and sometimes it is hard to say if we are the masters or the slaves. As an example, Facebook was valued at more than $150 two years ago and it has improved substantially since then (Truong 2015). The question is, do the users own Facebook or does Facebook own the users? This delicate balance is a co-evolution between humans and technology and in the future the balance will be between humans and artificial intelligence. We cannot deny the massive changes taking place in our society, to which humans must adjust rapidly and must do so until these co-evolutionary relationships stabilize. With previous technology man has had a lifetime, generations, decades, or years to respond but now we have less and less time to adjust.

The New Life Cycle

The model where you could consume a lifetime's worth of learning in the first few years of life and for the rest of life draw down on that depositary until retirement is entirely gone. Now the model is work and learn and work and learn. The old model was to start work and then to work until the end of your working life and retire. That is not very useful anymore because in five years of working the fundamental knowledge-driven skill is outdated. What we know is no longer going to be correct. To foster this individual, corporate, and societal evolution we must adopt the creation of mechanisms for continued education and continued learning. It should be understood that workers think, reflect, introspect, sympathize, empathize, relate, cooperate, plot, strategize, etc. and learn quite naturally. However, attention must be paid to the changing dynamics of the environment and its ever changing workplace requirement. Otherwise, a worker becomes obsolete and is no longer able to function effectively in the workforce. If a worker leaves the workplace and stays out for any period, the skills required to re-enter will have changed and the older skills no longer relevant with the latest trends. The longer a worker is out the more difficult reconnecting will be. Every year out of the workforce represents five years of learning lost. For workers, staying in the game is going to be important which creates more pressure on individuals to keep their skills current and continually update those skills.

Big changes are upon us personally, organizationally, and societally. In addition, there are no rules. The rules we grew up with, the ones we understood about how to run businesses, companies, countries, or politics are changing and if we keep going back to rules that we knew worked only a few years ago, we will find that they are useless now. There are no longer benchmarks of comparison, no rules of thumb, and no crib notes hidden away. The challenge is to learn to live in the moment and to engage the moment on its own terms with no reference to irrelevant rules.

What should a Worker Do?

There are four distinct things that workers need to become good at, namely: learning, mastering, connecting, and pivoting. Learning enables staying relevant in today's workplace. It is learning by doing and not learning by reading. Reading about artificial intelligence until you think you understand it provides only an abstract view. To learn about artificial intelligence it needs to be dabbled in, messed around with, and hacked around with to understand and build personal intuition. Learning must be done by making mistakes. All learning is full of failures that teach something and enables movement to the next thing.

Mastery has several dimensions. There is mastery of one's self or knowing one's spiritual, emotional, and physical center. This involves mastery of the art of telling your own story and mastery of changing that story as times and environments change. It is mastery of your own ability to hold your attention and master your moods and how to embody your learning. Initial learning is in the head but acting on that knowledge sometimes requires that the head get out of the way and allow intuition, heart, and body to take charge. Today we start work by opening an email, but then something pops up and we open another browser tab, and remember some other forgotten thing, another tab opens up, somebody calls, WhatsApp on the phone, then to coffee break, and when we return to our desk, we wonder where we started. Attention spans have diminished in this environment. On one hand technology is distracting us and making our attention spans lower and on the other hand it is taking away jobs that require lower attention spans. Workers must learn to draw from their own energy and intelligence rather than just pure knowledge.

The next stage level of mastery is the mastery of relationships. This is really about learning empathy. A lot of the work of a human involves motivating, managing, or collaboration with other people to get things done. To be effective and efficient, the process requires some knowledge of people's wants and to be able to frame interaction in a way that helps other people to see, understand, and have some affinity for the project. This does not come simply from words but involves the time and energy to create a transparent, secure, comfortable, and interactive relationship.

Learning and mastery drive the third skill of connecting. A person's ability to think clearly about learning and mastery of themselves, their abilities, and relationships results in a connective state. The basic "personal" platform quite naturally leads to connecting with people, companies, and technologies. Knowing yourself allows you to know others.

Finally, the ability to pivot embodies the idea and recognition that, whether we like it or not, things will change. To be valued and viable in the workplace workers must lean into the change and not resist it. This involves the process of embracing change by making it work for you by continually updating and learning skills and telling their new story every time something changes. The ability to pivot may be the most relevant and important ability. If we hold on to dogmas or beliefs that are never questioned we will be misaligned to these changing times.

Human Versus Machine

In the previous iteration of the industrial revolution it paid to have people work and think like machines. They showed up at the office at a certain time of the day and worked for eight, ten, 12 hours, and they went home. The worker was essentially a cog in the wheel of a large industrial machine. That model has almost disappeared. Today people are plugged in all the time, work from anywhere, and at any time. They never unplug. They always have this low level of engagement with devices and are never able to step away from the work day. The need today and in the future is not for humans to be more machine-like or for companies to be more machine-like, it is for humans to be more human-like. How strong can a human become physically? Machines are routinely created that are stronger than a person. It does not help humans to aspire to be physically stronger. How about working long hours? If a worker is working eight hours at some level of productivity is it reasonable to assume that in 12 hours they will be 50 percent more productive or 100 percent, or 300 percent? Productivity is not directly correlated to the hours of work you put in.

The revelation is that human beings are not machines but machines are becoming more human-like. They are cognitively capable of doing relatively simple tasks originally carried out by human workers. It was not so long ago that the word computer itself referred to human beings and not computers. Maybe knowledge workers will essentially become software robots in the future. The point is that tasks that can be automated *will* be automated.

There's nothing immoral about it; this is how the process works. What are human beings going to do after that? This is the point at which we look back at the master-slave conversation presented earlier. We will either be the slave and be told to fill the last mile of connectivity between what a computer can do and what human beings can do—take this box out of the autonomous truck and deliver to the spot where the drone will pick it up. Alternatively, we become masters of technology and use the technology like we are able to use fire or language or money.

The Never Ending Distractions

The negative dynamics of technology are only present because humans have not learned to live with technology and still retain control of our own senses. We are now being more and more distracted and aren't able to unplug long enough for our roots to regenerate and for our hearts to recover, and for our minds to seek reason and truth on any subject. This co-evolution with technology, as technology becomes more sophisticated, will involve learning to grow in tune with it. For example, think about we can pick up a book and read it without having to think about the act of reading. Reading is not innate, it is something we are trained to do. We learn the alphabet and how it sounds. We put the sounds together and learn how to read words, then sentences, paragraphs, books, and eventually gain fluency. We then can talk about them, which is another learned skill. These things are things that we can learn just the same as technology can be learned. Existing technologies, artificial intelligence, machine intelligence, automation, autonomous machines, and whatever else appears is something we have to learn to live with. We have to evolve ourselves and our social systems to be in sync with new technologies just as we have with technologies since the dawn of man. There is every reason to be optimistic about a future in which the human can become the master. Once again we will have an opportunity for all humans to be less machine-like and more human-like, live more fulfilling, prosperous, and satisfying lives. We have to learn to be human again and that is a great future to look forward to.

References

Loehr, J. and Schwartz, T. (2001). "The Making of a Corporate Athlete." *Harvard Business Review*. Available at: https://hbr.org/2001/01/the-making-of-a-corporate-athlete.

Truong, A. (2015). "Valuation of Various Tech Companies Per User." *Quartz*. Available at: https://www.theatlas.com/charts/N1QFzlXv.

19

Entrepreneurship as the New Driver of Business

Entrepreneurship has enabled newcomers to successfully challenge existing large corporations during the transition from the industrial to the digital era. Entrepreneurs take their creations online instantly instead of the conventional method of starting in a local geography and expanding into international markets. Digital economy, globalization, and entrepreneurship have become interwoven factors. With the support of capital from venture capital funds, they are not only driving a creative destruction of existing business for developing new things, but also developing new business models, ideas to make new products, and developing new technologies. Silicon Valley provides an example of an ecosystem required for successfully breeding entrepreneurship with its education system with cutting-edge research, culture, acceptance of failure, and availability of finance. Entrepreneurial development in the digital age has moved from development of hardware and software platforms, to the creation of, and access to, the technology platforms, and to the development of new business models. Replication of new business models is now almost instantaneous.

As we have looked at the history, geography, and legacy of globalization, a recurring theme has emerged around the topic of entrepreneurship. In the first chapter we thought about e-commerce as a tool for empowering individual entrepreneurship, and many large corporations use of e-commerce or e-business for international marketing of their products and services. In Chapter 8 we looked at the entrepreneurial energy in emerging economies and the prominence of this energy in India in Chapter 10. This hot topic and its disruptive influence and value for the global business are the focus of this chapter's discussion.

What is Entrepreneurship?

Entrepreneurship is not a new term, but it has become a key player in the technologically connected world. The contribution and value of entrepreneurs is a part of the legacy of business. The term entrepreneurship was coined around the 1920s, but the original word entrepreneur has its roots in eighteenth-century France, from "*entreprendre*" to "undertake" (Oxford 2017). It came to prominence in the English vocabulary in the first part of the twentieth century, being used to describe the creative destruction that involves replacement and creation. This creative destruction was largely responsible for much of the economic growth in the early 1900s with, for example, a new look at the steam engine and the horse carriage. An innovative combination of the two gave birth to today's automotive industry. This creative destruction not only created new things but also using a new eye to combine ideas in unique ways to make new products and technologies.

This disruption both spawned and exacerbated the digital explosion that has fundamentally change the business model. Robert Reich, Chancellor's Professor of Public Policy at the University of California Berkeley and Senior Fellow at the Blum Center for Developing Economies, defines an entrepreneur as someone who has leadership and management ability, and above all, the ability to build a team. This suggests that entrepreneurship is the capacity to see things differently from a different perspective. It is not simply about starting a business and managing its resources but seeing those resources in different ways that make them more effective and produce new value chains attractive to whole new markets. While entrepreneurial businesses may be small businesses, they are not "just" small businesses. Many small businesses tend to focus on existing products where there is stable demand, an established market, and a standardized business model. They are one of many that supply the market and are small businesses in the classical sense. The entrepreneurial business looks at the hotel model and at the technological market, say, and comes up with an Airbnb innovation that changes the industry model and turns it on its head. The entrepreneurial organization looks at the same set of conditions as anyone else but sees the hidden possibilities and inserts creative disruption.

The idea that entrepreneurship is restricted to smaller companies is a myth. Entrepreneurship is also a big company thing with its own nomenclature, "Intrapreneurship." Entrepreneurs working inside large corporations have both positive and negative elements. Positively, many of the infrastructure systems needed already exist inside the organization, and negatively, those same systems can be barriers to change. Entrepreneurship is a state of mind. It is a way to figure out with limited resources, how to create something new, something of value, and change the world. Intrapreneurship tied to corporate ventures, or large entities is alive and well. Entrepreneurship is not just about big business, smaller businesses, and start-ups but rather, it is a mindset, a state of mind that organizations need to possess to be valuable in the future.

Key to Success

There are several recognized entrepreneurial communities around the world like Tel Aviv, Singapore, Netherlands, Bangalore, and Silicon Valley (Compass 2015). These are places that seem to excel at enabling the blossoming of entrepreneurship. What is the secret of these "meccas" and can they be duplicated?

There seems to be a bit of common wisdom here. Entrepreneurship succeeds because of the ecosystem around it. The system should have world-class universities with cutting edge research, new ideas, and open environments. It needs access to, and availability of, capital through alternative source as many financial centers do not always foster entrepreneurship. Capital access requires the third leg of the stool to function properly. This third leg is the willingness of people to take risks. This is a basic recognition that failure is not a negative. In Silicon Valley, for example, failure is viewed as a positive necessity of success. More lessons are learned from failures than from success, and rather than rejecting it, Silicon Valley tends to embrace it. This type of ecosystem creates an environment of opportunity and an enabling space that allows for the mitigation of barriers that, though well intentioned, are a means of maintaining old business models and old paradigms.

These centers do not go unnoticed and experience an ever-increasing stream of supplicants. Their question is always the same, "Can this phenomena be replicated in my local community?" The answer is yes but not by copying Silicon Valley or any other successful centers. Trying to replicate Silicon Valley does not work because every local community is not Silicon Valley. What does work is understanding how the local environment is unique. Examining what it thrives on and excels at, how involved people are, and how people can become more involved. Local communities must create their own entrepreneurial culture around the core elements of existing successful parameters; that is, strong educational institutions, access to creative capital, and the willingness to take risks. It has little to do with rules and regulations because governments often get in the way of entrepreneurship.

Why Become an Entrepreneur?

The top four reasons why people become an entrepreneur are money, flexibility, control, and the desire to leave a legacy. The most entrepreneurial countries per capita are Uganda with 28.1 percent, Thailand with 16.7 percent, Brazil with 13.8 percent, Cameroon with 13.7 percent, and Vietnam with 13.3 percent. The top three most funded industries in entrepreneurship start-ups are software, media and entertainment, and biotechnology (Brinded 2015).

A key point to remember is that entrepreneurship is a way of thinking, a different view of the world, a different spirit. Interestingly some of the most successful entrepreneurs come from developing countries or emerging nations. The presence of technological interconnectivity is enabling constant improvement with more entrepreneurs understanding the business environment, how to create disruptive innovation, and how to thrive in their environments. This also has an egalitarian effect whether readily accepted by governments or forced upon them. These markets reap the benefit of the evolution of creative disruption. The first phase of entrepreneurial development in the information technology space was the creation of hardware and software. Companies like Microsoft and Apple were the first generation creators that built the hardware and software platforms for today's business. The second phase was creation of access by the general populace to the technology platforms and the global stage. Companies like Google and Facebook built new business models around evolving hardware and software. The third phase is the technology industry's focus on developing new business models. Examples are Uber as a worldwide taxi service in the United States. China picked up the idea as Didi, and India as Ola Cabs. Replication of new business models can be almost instantaneous.

These new business models, while having a disrupting effect on old paradigms, also have the effect of creating new paradigms ripe for disruption. For example technology has facilitated direct access to consumers and abolished the need for intermediaries yet businesses like Facebook and Google have become the new middlemen. They do not own any information but instead provide direct resources that people put to work. Amazon is a classic market middleman that primarily becomes the connector cable between sellers and buyers. The Internet removed the old middlemen and replaced them with new ones. The takeaway here is that this evolution will never have a resting place, but just as one model has disrupted with its creativity, it will become the next target of further creative disruption. Just as we have seen many physical retailers disappear from the market over the past decade, we will see creative destruction affect technology companies as well.

The availability of cellular services and smartphones around the world has had a profound impact on the consumer market. A consumer with money to spend can be accessed through a smartphone anywhere in the world. In the old paradigm, the entrepreneur would select the target market and demographic and begin, over time, to penetrate and be absorbed by consumers in that market. Today the entrepreneur puts a product, service, or application onto the Internet with virtually no control over that consumer's access to the offering. This means businesses have to start thinking differently. Everything has changed, customer demand, supply chains, shipping channels, product characteristics, everything. Every business today is a global business from day one whether the product is digital or not. If it is available online, it is accessible by consumers everywhere.

References

Brinded, L. (2015). "The 9 Countries with the Most Entrepreneurship." *Business Insider*. Available at: http://www.businessinsider.com/top-9-countries-with-the-largest-amount-of-entrepreneurs-2015-6/#chile–this-country-is-considered-one-of-south-americas-most-stable-and-prosperous-nations-and-about-11-of-its-population-choose-entrepreneurship-here-a-big-seminar-on-chile-based-startups-is-underway-1.

Compass (2015). "The Global Startup Ecosystem Ranking 2015." *Global Startup Ecosystem Ranking*.

Oxford English Dictionary (2017). Oxford: Oxford University Press. Available at: https://en.oxforddictionaries.com/definition/entrepreneur.

20

The Future of Globalization

Is globalization under attack? The current geopolitical environment is indicating a shift toward protectionism, nationalism, and isolationism. The US elections and Brexit are a reflection of public sentiments. It will be interesting to see how much the current rhetoric is able to dent globalization, which has become an integral part of our society because of technological interconnectedness. Globalization has been underway for centuries with trade, entertainment, cuisines, education, and politics. Today physical interconnectivity has been replaced by digital connectivity. There are more than 350 million cross-border e-commerce shoppers. In 2015 almost 244 million people were living away from their home country, and around 40 million were crossing borders for work. There are nearly 400 million international travelers every year (Minges 2016).

History

The initial axiom to understand is that politics and economics cannot be separated. Those who attempt to do so have paid a heavy price. Therefore, if the consequences are known and the globalization phenomenon universally evident than what causes the kind of push back in terms of public discourse and political rhetoric? To understand this phenomenon let's look at the history of globalization after the Second World War. What has been the history of global trade in product, services, information, and knowledge? Since the mid-1950s some countries have created an unfair advantage for their domestic companies in the form of subsidies, tax breaks, and low interest rates. These countries are enabling competition for their domestic companies in foreign markets. This unfair advantage or unfair competition is in direct conflict with the domestic companies from foreign markets. Those domestic enterprises are often outpriced and pushed out of the market with the likely loss of jobs. An example of this is the steel industry. The industry suffered from oversupply after the entry of new producers in the 1970s. That oversupply, primarily driven by geopolitical tariff and non-tariff strategies, had significant ramifications on the industry. This was not only in terms of workforce reduction but also innovation and the introduction of automation powered by the competitive nature of the environment. In the past 25 years the steel industry workforce around the world has been reduced by 1.5 million workers (West 2015).

Strategies to Create an Advantage

Some countries employ a limited, or no regulatory framework to the point where firms do not pay much attention to issues like worker safety, health, and human rights. The objective in these countries is to keep the labor cost low and to compete in foreign markets, regardless of endangering workers. In the garment stitching industry there are many cases of factories catching fire and industrial accidents where hundreds of workers have died. Countries where environmental laws are not rigorously enforced allow businesses to destroy the environment simply in order to produce goods at low cost.

Countries have imposed high tariffs or raised non-tariff barriers to protect their own domestic firms. At the same time, they push direct exports to other nations. Countries will also adopt weak currency policies, known as devaluation, to compete with low-cost goods and boost their exports. Global trade has benefited several countries who do not play by the rules.

These unfair practices adversely affect countries' sensitivity to employment and human rights, environmental rights, and transparent financial, or market-based currency policies. The push back that is happening in the United States, United Kingdom, and to some extent in Europe is unlikely to reverse this trend. In the long term, there is little chance of a return to the protectionist policies of the past. However, there will be some course correction that will facilitate the continuation of globalization as a fairer game.

The Enablers

It is worth remembering that apart from the obvious negative economic focus on globalization, today's world is "normatively" global. Globalization has been happening for centuries and millennia. Cultures have been globalizing. People have been traveling from one country to another country. Popular cuisines travel all over the world. Hollywood and Bollywood entertainment is everywhere. There is a globalization of education, politics, and society. It is not just confined to global trade, and we need to understand that this connectedness and interdependence are expanding. Historically, culture and social forces have been traveling from one country to another through physical contact but today times are different. Digital interconnectedness has made this connection instantaneous and normal. So as long as physical and digital interconnectedness exists and societies and people's lives improve, the potential of reduction in the scope of globalism is unlikely. However, the way the game is played will change. Indeed, it must change.

The Political Agenda

Regardless of the staying power of globalization, the re-emergence of an old ideology in the United States and Europe has sent a shiver across the globe. Could this be the time when protectionism's impact will change everything? The risk of automobile companies being forced to adopt a different model of producing cars, or the disruption of the supply chains in the pharmaceutical industry is almost unimaginable. A realistic view of the world leads to an understanding that nationalism and protectionism are the lenses of the past. Twenty-first-century integration of societies, cultures, and economics cannot use nineteenth- and twentieth-century ways of thinking. New paradigms that support the fair distribution of benefit must define and infuse global trade. Even in the midst of jargon-laced rhetoric such as Made in America, Make America Great Again, Made in India, and Brexit, uses thinking that looks backward rather than forward. Slogans like "Make America/ the United Kingdom/India great again" reflect a great sentiment to share in the public space. Pride in one's country is a commendable sentiment. However, what does such an emotive slogan like make the nation great again really mean? What kind of greatness? Great military power? A great geopolitical power? A great economic power? A great social and cultural power? Is it greatness from the point of view of decision makers, students of anthropology, or students of the evolution of societies? Unless there is clarity regarding the definition, the slogan becomes meaningless.

The prevalent, though less heard, view of what is now becoming a universal political agenda is being seen in the political priorities of countries around the world. Conversations are about healthcare, providing nutrition and affordable housing, transforming school education, reducing unemployment and creating new jobs, upgrading infrastructure, protecting the environment, providing power, water, and sanitation, and creating smart, caring, and transparent governments. This is the predominant language of politicians in most countries. This is what society is asking for and, if political leaders are sincere and if societies can exert pressure on their political leaders, this is going to become the next force regarding globalization.

It is likely that the next round of globalization will not just focus on providing consumer products, rather, it will expand the social sector addressed by conversations on healthcare, providing nutrition, affordable housing, and the like. This emphasis will unleash a new wave of globalization across the world. There is current evidence of cooperation between countries and companies in the areas of energy, water, and sanitation. Countries coming together to solve the problem of nutrition leads to an opportunity for a great exchange of goods and services.

Digital Connectivity

Digital connectivity has done something absolutely remarkable. It has changed the way new international players are emerging in the marketplace. In the past, start-ups were small and domestic and would grow bigger in their own country of origin. At a certain size, they took the first step to expanding into foreign markets and over a period of time grew into international and multinational companies. Through digital interconnectedness, an individual can now access global markets immediately. Individuals meanwhile are exploiting the power of digital interconnectedness in terms of socializing, exchanging opinions and information, buying and selling goods, learning from each other, educating each other, and entertainment. A musician who is positioned to upload creative, entertainment products can expect people to pay and download their music no matter where they are. The domain of individual entrepreneurs is going to expand dramatically. The numbers are rising exponentially. This is the age of DICE, "digitally interconnected entrepreneurs." Today you do not have to be a big multinational to be able to reach customers in far corners of the global market, you just have to want to do it.

What Has Changed?

Where at one time we fought over shipping lanes, industrial sites, or the sourcing of raw material, now the substitute is broadband and the demand for intangibles. There are no restrictions to participating in the global economy through the Internet. We have places like Pinkoi, a collection of 20,000 independent designers who are offering their products online from Taiwan. Or Amazon, with almost 2 million sellers and Alibaba with 10 million merchants that are as close as your screen. There are 914 million Internet users with at least one foreign social connection. There are almost 400 million international travelers every year. There are around 350 million cross-border e-commerce shoppers. It is likely that an order from the United States will be shipped from Beijing or Bangalore or Philippines or Vietnam. In 2015, almost 200 million people were living away from their home country, and around 40 million were crossing borders for work. There were 12 million online students who are studying across borders and 5 million students studying abroad (Manyika et al. 2016).

The world has benefited from the US growth in the last 50 years because they and Europe were the engines of growth around the world. Today, however, the driving engine of global growth from the economics viewpoint is not the triad countries (namely, the United States, Japan, and Europe), it is emerging economies. There remains a strong interdependence in the sense that emerging markets cannot grow on their own. They have to depend on a symbiotic relationship between the triad countries. The whole paradigm of growth is about winning together, rather than one country leading and the rest following, and globalization continues to be key to the successful growth of the global economy.

References

Manyika, J., Lund, S., Bughin, J., Woetzel, J., Stamenov, K., and Dhingra, D. (2016). *Digital Globalization: The Era of Global Flows*. Mckinsey Global Institute Report.

Minges, M. (2016). *In Search of Cross-Border e-Commerce Trade Data*. United Nations Conference on Trade and Development.

West, D. M. (2015). "What Happens if Robots Take the Jobs? The Impact of Emerging Technologies on Employment and Public Policy." *Center for Technology Innovation at Brookings*. Available at: https://www.brookings.edu/wp-content/uploads/2016/06/robotwork.pdf.

Index